Language: Usage and Practice, Grade 7

Contents

Contents continued

Contents *continued*

Unit 4: Capitalization and Punctuation

Unit 5: Composition

Unit 6: Study Skills

AF207608

The *Language: Usage and Practice* series meets many needs.

- ▣ It is designed for students who require additional practice in the basics of effective writing and speaking.
- ▣ It provides focused practice in key grammar, usage, mechanics, and composition areas.
- ▣ It helps students gain ownership of essential skills.
- ▣ It presents practice exercises in a clear, concise format in a logical sequence.
- ▣ It allows for easy and independent use.

The *Language: Usage and Practice* lessons are organized into a series of units arranged in a logical sequence.

- ▣ vocabulary ▣ sentences ▣ grammar and usage
- ▣ mechanics of capitalization and punctuation ▣ composition skills

The *Language: Usage and Practice* lessons are carefully formatted for student comfort.

- ▣ Systematic, focused attention is given to just one carefully selected skill at a time.
- ▣ Rules are clearly stated at the beginning of each lesson and are illustrated with examples.
- ▣ Key terms are introduced in bold type.
- ▣ Meaningful practice exercises reinforce the skill.
- ▣ Each lesson is clearly labeled, and directions are clear and uncomplicated.

The *Language: Usage and Practice* series stresses the application of language principles in a variety of ways.

- ▣ Students are asked to match, circle, or underline elements in a predetermined sentence.
- ▣ Students are also asked to use what they have learned in an original sentence or in rewriting a sentence.

The *Language: Usage and Practice* series is designed for independent use.

- ☐ Because the format is logical and consistent and the vocabulary is carefully controlled, students can use *Language: Usage and Practice* with a high degree of independence.
- ☐ Copies of the worksheets can be given to individuals, pairs of students, or small groups for completion.
- ☐ Worksheets can be used in the language arts center.
- ☐ Worksheets can be given as homework for reviewing and reinforcing skills.

The *Language: Usage and Practice* series provides writing instruction.

- ☐ The process approach to teaching writing provides success for most students.
- ☐ *Language: Usage and Practice* provides direct support for the teaching of composition and significantly enhances those strategies and techniques commonly associated with the process-writing approach.
- ☐ Each book includes a composition unit that provides substantial work with composition skills, such as writing topic sentences, selecting supporting details, taking notes, writing reports, and revising and proofreading.
- ☐ Also included in the composition unit is practice with various prewriting activities, such as clustering and brainstorming, which play an important part in process writing.
- ☐ The composition lessons are presented in the same rule-plus-practice format as in the other units.

The *Language: Usage and Practice* series includes additional features.

- ☐ **Unit Tests**   Use the unit tests to check student progress and prepare students for standardized tests.
- ☐ **Sequential Support**   The content of each unit is repeated and expanded in subsequent levels as highlighted in the skills correlation chart on pages 5 and 6.
- ☐ **Assessment**   Use the Assessment on pages 7–10 to determine the skills your students need to practice.
- ☐ **Language Terms**   Provide each student with a copy of the list of language terms on the inside back cover to keep for reference throughout the year.
- ☐ **Small-Group Activities**   Use the worksheets as small-group activities to give students the opportunity to work cooperatively.

The *Language: Usage and Practice* series is a powerful tool!

**The activities use a variety of strategies to maintain student interest.
Watch your students' language improve as skills are
applied in structured, relevant practice!**

Skills Correlation

	1	2	3	4	5	6	7	8	High School
Vocabulary									
Rhyming Words	■	■							
Synonyms and Antonyms	■	■	■	■	■	■	■	■	■
Homonyms	■	■	■	■	■	■	■	■	■
Multiple Meanings/Homographs	■	■	■	■	■	■	■	■	■
Prefixes and Suffixes			■	■	■	■	■	■	■
Compound Words			■	■	■	■	■	■	■
Contractions		■	■	■	■	■	■	■	■
Idioms						■	■	■	■
Connotation/Denotation					■	■	■	■	
Sentences									
Word Order in Sentences	■	■		■					
Recognizing Sentences and Sentence Types	■	■	■	■	■	■	■	■	■
Subjects and Predicates	■	■	■	■	■	■	■	■	■
Compound/Complex Sentences			■	■	■	■	■	■	■
Sentence Combining		■	■	■	■	■	■	■	■
Run-on Sentences			■	■	■	■	■	■	■
Independent and Subordinate Clauses							■	■	■
Compound Subjects and Predicates	■			■	■	■	■	■	■
Direct and Indirect Objects					■		■	■	■
Inverted Word Order						■	■	■	■
Grammar and Usage									
Common and Proper Nouns	■	■	■	■	■	■	■	■	■
Singular and Plural Nouns	■	■	■	■	■	■	■	■	■
Possessive Nouns			■	■	■	■	■	■	
Appositives						■	■	■	
Verbs and Verb Tense	■	■	■	■	■	■	■	■	■
Regular/Irregular Verbs	■	■	■	■	■	■	■	■	■
Subject/Verb Agreement	■	■	■	■	■	■	■	■	■
Verb Phrases						■	■	■	■
Transitive and Intransitive Verbs							■	■	
Verbals: Gerunds, Participles, and Infinitives							■	■	■
Active and Passive Voice							■	■	
Mood								■	
Pronouns	■	■	■	■	■	■	■	■	■
Antecedents						■	■	■	■
Articles	■	■	■		■	■			
Adjectives	■	■	■	■	■	■	■	■	■
Correct Word Usage (e.g., may/can, sit/set)	■		■	■	■	■	■	■	■
Adverbs			■	■	■	■	■	■	■
Prepositions						■	■	■	■
Prepositional Phrases						■	■	■	■
Conjunctions						■	■	■	■
Interjections						■	■		
Double Negatives								■	■
Capitalization and Punctuation									
Capitalization: First Word in Sentence	■	■	■	■	■	■	■	■	■
Capitalization: Proper Nouns	■	■	■	■	■	■	■	■	■
Capitalization: in Letters		■	■	■		■	■	■	■
Capitalization: Abbreviations and Titles		■	■	■	■	■	■	■	■
Capitalization: Proper Adjectives					■	■	■	■	■

	1	2	3	4	5	6	7	8	High School
Capitalization and Punctuation (cont'd)									
End Punctuation	■	■	■	■	■	■	■	■	■
Commas		■	■	■	■	■	■	■	■
Apostrophes in Contractions		■	■	■	■	■	■	■	■
Apostrophes in Possessives			■	■	■	■	■	■	■
Quotation Marks			■	■	■	■	■	■	■
Colons/Semicolons					■	■	■	■	■
Hyphens						■	■	■	■
Composition									
Expanding Sentences		■		■	■	■	■		
Paragraphs: Topic Sentence (main idea)		■	■	■	■	■	■	■	■
Paragraphs: Supporting Details		■	■	■	■	■	■	■	■
Order in Paragraphs		■	■	■		■	■		
Writing Process:									
Audience				■	■	■	■	■	
Topic			■	■	■	■	■	■	
Outlining				■		■	■	■	
Clustering/Brainstorming					■		■	■	
Note Taking						■			
Revising/Proofreading					■	■	■	■	
Types of Writing:									
Poem	■								
Letter	■	■	■			■			
"How-to" Paragraph			■						
Invitation			■						
Telephone Message			■						
Conversation				■					
Narrative Paragraph				■					
Comparing and Contrasting					■				
Descriptive Paragraph					■				
Report						■			
Interview							■		
Persuasive Composition								■	
Readiness/Study Skills									
Grouping	■		■						
Letters of Alphabet	■								
Listening	■	■							
Making Comparisons	■	■							
Organizing Information		■	■						
Following Directions	■	■	■	■	■				
Alphabetical Order	■	■	■	■	■				
Using a Dictionary:									
Definitions		■	■			■	■	■	
Guide Words/Entry Words		■	■	■	■	■	■	■	
Syllables and Pronunciation					■	■	■	■	
Multiple Meanings		■	■			■	■	■	
Word Origins						■	■	■	
Parts of a Book		■				■			
Using the Library						■	■	■	
Using Encyclopedias				■	■	■	■	■	
Using Reference Books						■	■	■	
Using the *Readers' Guide*							■	■	
Using Tables, Charts, Graphs, and Diagrams								■	
Choosing Appropriate Sources						■	■	■	

Skills Correlation
Language: Usage and Practice 7, SV 1419027840

Assessment

✳ **Write S before each pair of synonyms, A before each pair of antonyms, and H before each pair of homonyms.**

_____ **1.** board, bored   _____ **3.** antique, ancient

_____ **2.** tall, short   _____ **4.** massive, huge

✳ **Write the homograph for the pair of meanings.**

5. _____ **a.** a piece of hair   **b.** to fasten securely

✳ **Write P before each word with a prefix, S before each word with a suffix, and C before each compound word.**

_____ **6.** overcome   _____ **8.** rusty

_____ **7.** misplace   _____ **9.** disinterested

✳ **Write the words that make up each contraction.**

10. they'll _____ _____   **11.** we've _____ _____

✳ **Underline the word in parentheses that has the more positive connotation.**

12. The (crabby, unhappy) child squirmed in her mother's arms.

✳ **Circle the letter of the idiom that means to suddenly become angry.**

13. a. put up with   **b.** fly off the handle

✳ **Write D before the declarative sentence, IM before the imperative sentence, E before the exclamatory sentence, and IN before the interrogative sentence. Then underline the simple subject and circle the simple predicate in each sentence.**

_____ **14.** Wait until the speech is over.   _____ **16.** Ouch! I burned myself!

_____ **15.** What do you believe?   _____ **17.** That article really made me angry.

✳ **Write CS before the sentence that has a compound subject and CP before the sentence that has a compound predicate.**

_____ **18.** He stumbled and fell on the rough ground.

_____ **19.** Carmen and Jasper are the leading actors.

✳ **Write CS before the compound sentence. Write RO before the run-on sentence. Write I before the sentence that is in inverted order.**

_____ **20.** Through the woods ran the frightened deer.

_____ **21.** Once she had lived in New York, she lives in Toronto now.

_____ **22.** Brenda was cold, so she built a roaring fire.

✳ **Put brackets around the subordinate clause and underline the independent clause in this complex sentence. Then write DO above the direct object.**

23. Before I left, I ate a good breakfast.

Assessment, p. 2

✳ **Underline the common nouns and circle the proper nouns in the sentence.**

24. Mayor Dumonte showed the citizens of our city that he was honest by appointing Ms. Lopez to the position.

✳ **Circle the appositive in the sentence. Underline the noun it identifies or explains.**

25. His favorite nurse, Ms. Abram, made his stay in the hospital more pleasant.

✳ **Write past, present, or future to show the tense of each underlined verb.**

_____ **26.** We will have the best seats in the house.

_____ **27.** The actors prepare for months beforehand.

_____ **28.** Critics described this play as one of the best ever.

✳ **Circle the correct verbs in parentheses to complete each sentence.**

29. Here (is, are) the paper clips you (were, was) asking for.

30. She (seen, saw) her brother before he (know, knew) she was there.

31. It had (begun, began) to rain, so he (gone, went) inside.

32. She (thrown, threw) the dish and (broken, broke) it.

✳ **Circle the letter of the sentence that is in the active voice.**

33. a. The letter was received a day late.

b. Jerratt sent his package in overnight mail.

✳ **Write SP before the sentence that has a subject pronoun, OP before the sentence that has an object pronoun, PP before the sentence that has a possessive pronoun, and IP before the sentence that has an indefinite pronoun. Circle the pronoun in each sentence.**

_____ **34.** Somebody knows what happened.

_____ **35.** Rick wrote that poem for her.

_____ **36.** The band played their favorite song.

_____ **37.** We felt surprised and upset.

✳ **Underline the pronoun in the sentence. Circle its antecedent.**

38. The jets flew in their assigned formation.

✳ **On the line before each sentence, write adjective or adverb to describe the underlined word or words.**

_____ **39.** That farm is up for sale.

_____ **40.** The dog's yelps were extremely loud.

_____ **41.** She spoke more enthusiastically than anyone else.

_____ **42.** Some Mexican food is very spicy and hot.

✳ **Underline each prepositional phrase twice. Circle each preposition. Underline the conjunction once.**

43. The girl on the bus waved at me while it passed by.

Name _____ Date _____

Assessment, p. 3

 Rewrite the letter. Use capital letters and punctuation marks where needed.

956 e. garden circle
bowman tx 78787
april 13 2007

dear steve

were so excited youre coming to visit ____ even little scott managed to say uncle steve visit which was pretty good for a child of only twenty two months wouldnt you agree ____ oh i want to be sure i have the information correct ____ please let me know as soon as possible if any of this is wrong flight 561 arrives at 310 P.M. on may 22 ____ see you then ____

your sister
amanda

_____

_____

_____

_____

_____

_____

_____

_____

_____

_____

 Number the sentences in order, with the topic sentence first.

44. _____ Then the wool is combed and formed into neat rolls.

_____ Making wool thread by hand is a time-consuming art.

_____ The spinner goes to work making thread after the wool is combed.

_____ First, a sheep's wool is shaved off and cleaned.

 Circle the letter of the better interview question.

45. a. Is it your feeling that the city council's decision has failed the voters?

b. Why do you think that the mayor voted against the rest of the council?

Assessment, p. 4

✳ **Rewrite the sentence below. Correct the errors in the sentence by following the proofreader's marks.**

Although
46. the decision to to close mayfield park was unpoplar, proved it to be the correct choise.

_____

✳ **Use the dictionary entry to answer the questions.**

jolly (jäl´ē) *adj.* **1.** full of high spirits: joyous. **2.** expressing, suggesting, or inspiring gaiety: cheerful. [Middle English *joli*]

47. What part of speech is the word jolly? _____

48. Would jolly come before or after joust in the dictionary? _____

49. Which language is in the history of the word jolly? _____

50. Write jolly separated into syllables. _____

✳ **Write the source from the box that you would use to find the information listed.**

dictionary	encyclopedia	atlas	*Readers' Guide*

_____ 51. where to find an article in a certain magazine

_____ 52. a map of Europe

_____ 53. the etymology of the word lieutenant

_____ 54. an article on soapstone

✳ **Use the encyclopedia sample to answer the questions.**

CREE is the name of a Native American people now living on reservations in Canada. They were originally forest hunters and trappers who traded with the early French and English fur traders. Part of the group moved southwest into buffalo country and became known as Plains Cree. *See also* NATIVE AMERICANS.

55. What is the article about? _____

56. Where did these people originally get their food? _____

57. Where did some members of the tribe move? _____

58. Under what subject heading can you find related information? _____

Language: Usage and Practice 7, SV 1419027840

Synonyms and Antonyms

- A **synonym** is a word that has the same or nearly the same meaning as one or more other words.
  EXAMPLES: reply—answer   talk—speak

 Write a synonym for each word below.

1. pleasant _____
2. enough _____
3. leave _____
4. inquire _____

5. fearless _____
6. artificial _____
7. famous _____
8. trade _____

9. house _____
10. nation _____
11. difficult _____
12. vacant _____

 Write four sentences about recycling. In each sentence, use a synonym for the word in parentheses. Underline the synonym in your sentence.

13. (packaging) _____

14. (waste) _____

15. (landfill) _____

16. (planet) _____

- An **antonym** is a word that has the opposite meaning of another word.
  EXAMPLES: old—new   bad—good

 Write an antonym for each word below.

17. failure _____
18. absent _____
19. before _____
20. slow _____

21. all _____
22. forget _____
23. love _____
24. no _____

25. friend _____
26. always _____
27. light _____
28. forward _____

 In each sentence, write an antonym for the word in parentheses that makes sense in the sentence.

29. Thao ran his hand along the (smooth) _____ surface of the wood.

30. He knew he would have to (stop) _____ sanding it.

31. Only after sanding would he be able to (destroy) _____ a table.

32. He would try to (forget) _____ not to sand it too much.

Name _____ Date _____

Homonyms

• A **homonym** is a word that sounds the same as another word but has a different spelling and a different meaning.
EXAMPLES: aisle—I'll—isle   flower—flour

 Underline the correct homonym(s) in parentheses to complete each sentence.

1. The (two, too, to) people walked very slowly (passed, past) the house.

2. The children were (two, too, to) tired (two, too, to) talk.

3. Did you (hear, here) that noise?

4. Yes, I (heard, herd) it.

5. I do (knot, not) (know, no) of a person who is (knot, not) ready to help the hungry people of the world.

6. Michelle, you (seam, seem) to have forgotten about (our, hour) plans for the picnic.

7. Who (won, one) the citizenship (medal, meddle) this year?

8. Jim, how much do you (way, weigh)?

9. The night (air, heir) is (sew, so) cool that you will (knead, need) a light jacket.

10. The small plants were set out in orderly (rows, rose).

11. I (knew, new) those (knew, new) shoes would hurt my (feat, feet).

12. Which states lead in the production of (beat, beet) sugar?

13. We did (not, knot) go to the (seen, scene) of the wreck.

14. Shera wore the belt around her (waist, waste).

 Write a homonym for each word below.

15. peace _____	25. sew _____	35. knight _____
16. altar _____	26. break _____	36. hymn _____
17. to _____	27. week _____	37. through _____
18. way _____	28. rein _____	38. grown _____
19. beech _____	29. bare _____	39. wrap _____
20. plain _____	30. scene _____	40. prey _____
21. coarse _____	31. mite _____	41. strait _____
22. seem _____	32. whole _____	42. sole _____
23. knew _____	33. hoarse _____	43. hear _____
24. sale _____	34. fourth _____	44. ware _____

Unit 1: Vocabulary
Language: Usage and Practice 7, SV 1419027840

Homographs

> • A **homograph** is a word that has the same spelling as another word but a different meaning and sometimes a different pronunciation.
>   EXAMPLE: <u>saw</u>, meaning "have seen," and <u>saw</u>, meaning "a tool used for cutting"

 Circle the letter for the definition that best defines each underlined homograph.

1. Sara jumped at the <u>bangs</u> of the exploding balloons.

   a. fringe of hair   **b.** loud noises

2. She grabbed a stick to <u>arm</u> herself against the threat.

   a. part of the body   **b.** take up a weapon

3. The dog's <u>bark</u> woke the family.

   a. noise a dog makes   **b.** outside covering on a tree

4. Mix the pancake <u>batter</u> for three minutes.

   a. person at bat   **b.** mixture for cooking

 Use the homographs in the box to complete the sentences below. Each homograph will be used twice.

5. Pieces of a board game are _____.

   People who are cashiers are _____.

6. A water bird is a _____.

   To lower the head is to _____.

7. A metal container is a _____.

   If you are able, you _____.

8. To get down from something is to _____.

   If something is on fire, it is _____.

duck
alight
can
checkers

 Write the homograph for each pair of meanings below. The first letter of each word is given for you.

9. **a.** place for horses   **b.** delay   s _____

10. **a.** a metal fastener   **b.** a sound made with fingers   s _____

11. **a.** to crush   **b.** a yellow vegetable   s _____

12. **a.** a bad doctor   **b.** the sound made by a duck   q _____

13. **a.** to strike   **b.** a party fruit drink   p _____

www.harcourtschoolsupply.com

13

Unit 1: Vocabulary
Language: Usage and Practice 7, SV 1419027840

Prefixes

- A **prefix** added to the beginning of a base word changes the meaning of the word.

  EXAMPLE: dis, meaning "opposite of," + the base word <u>appear</u> = <u>disappear</u>, meaning "the opposite of appear"

  EXAMPLES:

prefix	meaning	prefix	meaning
in	not	re	again
dis	not	fore	before
un	not	pre	before
trans	across	mis	wrong
		with	from, against

 Write a new word using one of the prefixes listed above. Then write the meaning of the new word.

WORD	NEW WORD	MEANING
1. fair	_____	_____
2. justice	_____	_____
3. tell	_____	_____
4. warn	_____	_____
5. visible	_____	_____
6. spell	_____	_____
7. agree	_____	_____
8. see	_____	_____
9. behave	_____	_____
10. stand	_____	_____
11. complete	_____	_____
12. please	_____	_____
13. drawn	_____	_____
14. likely	_____	_____
15. match	_____	_____
16. clean	_____	_____
17. understand	_____	_____
18. correct	_____	_____

Language: Usage and Practice 7, SV 1419027840

Name _____ Date _____

Suffixes

- A **suffix** added to the end of a base word changes the meaning of the word.
  EXAMPLE: <u>less</u>, meaning "without," + the base word <u>worth</u> = <u>worthless</u>, meaning "without worth"

  EXAMPLES:

suffix	meaning	suffix	meaning
less	without	ist	one skilled in
ish	of the nature of	tion	art of
ous	full of	ful	full of
en	to make	al	pertaining to
hood	state of being	able	able to be
ward	in the direction of	ible	able to be
ness	quality of		

- Sometimes you need to change the spelling of a base word when a suffix is added.
  EXAMPLE: happy—happiness

 Write a new word using one of the suffixes listed above. Then write the meaning of the new word.

WORD	NEW WORD	MEANING
1. care	_____	_____
2. truth	_____	_____
3. fame	_____	_____
4. soft	_____	_____
5. down	_____	_____
6. light	_____	_____
7. east	_____	_____
8. honor	_____	_____
9. thank	_____	_____
10. rest	_____	_____
11. child	_____	_____
12. remark	_____	_____
13. violin	_____	_____
14. courage	_____	_____
15. worth	_____	_____

Language: Usage and Practice 7, SV 1419027840

Name _____   Date _____

Contractions

- A **contraction** is a word formed by joining two other words.
- An **apostrophe** shows where a letter or letters have been omitted.
    EXAMPLE: had not = hadn't
- <u>Won't</u> is an exception.
    EXAMPLE: will not = won't

 Write the contraction for each pair of words.

1. did not _____

2. was not _____

3. we are _____

4. is not _____

5. who is _____

6. had not _____

7. I will _____

8. I am _____

9. it is _____

10. do not _____

11. they have _____

12. would not _____

13. will not _____

14. does not _____

15. were not _____

16. there is _____

17. could not _____

18. I have _____

19. she will _____

20. they are _____

 Underline each contraction. Write the words that make up the contraction on the line.

21. They're dusting the piano very carefully before they inspect it. _____

22. They'll want to look closely, in case there are any scratches. _____

23. If it's in good condition, Mary will buy it. _____

24. Mary's an excellent piano player. _____

25. Her friends think she'll earn a college scholarship with her talent. _____

26. Thom doesn't play the piano, but he's a great cook. _____

27. He'd like to be a professional chef. _____

28. His friends would've liked for him to go to college. _____

29. But they aren't concerned as long as Thom's happy. _____

30. Thom and Mary think they've been lucky to have good friends. _____

Language: Usage and Practice 7, SV 1419027840

Name _____ Date _____

Compound Words

- A **compound word** is a word that is made up of two or more words.
- The meaning of many compound words is related to the meaning of each individual word.
    - EXAMPLE: blue + berry = blueberry, meaning "a type of berry that is blue in color"
- Compound words may be written as one word, as hyphenated words, or as two separate words. Always check a dictionary.

 Combine the words in the box to make compound words. You may use words more than once.

air	knob	door	port	paper	condition	black	berry
sand	line	stand	under	way	around	bird	sea

1. _____   7. _____

2. _____   8. _____

3. _____   9. _____

4. _____   10. _____

5. _____   11. _____

6. _____   12. _____

Answer the following questions.

13. Whirl means "to move in circles." What is a whirlpool?

_____

14. Something that is quick moves rapidly. What is quicksand?

_____

15. Rattle means "to make sharp, short sounds quickly." What is a rattlesnake?

_____

16. A ring is "a small, circular band." What is an earring?

_____

17. Pool can mean "a group of people who do something together." What is a carpool?

_____

18. A lace can be "a string or cord that is used to hold something together." What is a shoelace?

_____

Language: Usage and Practice 7, SV 1419027840

Name _____ Date _____

Connotation/Denotation

- The **denotation** of a word is its exact meaning as stated in a dictionary.
  EXAMPLE: The denotation of stingy is "ungenerous" or "miserly."
- The **connotation** of a word is an added meaning that suggests something positive or negative.
  EXAMPLES: **Negative:** Stingy suggests "ungenerous." Stingy has a negative connotation.
  Positive: Economical suggests "efficient" and "careful." Economical has a positive connotation.
- Some words are neutral. They do not suggest either good or bad feelings.
  EXAMPLES: garage   kitchen   roof

Write (–) if the underlined word has a negative connotation. Write (+) if it has a positive connotation. Write (N) if the word is neutral.

_____ 1. This is my house.

_____ 2. This is my home.

_____ 3. Darren's friends discussed his problem.

_____ 4. Darren's friends gossiped about his problem.

_____ 5. Our dog is sick.

_____ 6. Our dog is diseased.

_____ 7. The play was enjoyable.

_____ 8. The play was fantastic.

_____ 9. Julia is boring.

_____ 10. Julia is quiet.

Complete each sentence with the word that suggests the connotation given.

11. Our experience of the storm was _____. (negative)

12. Our experience of the storm was _____. (positive)

13. Our experience of the storm was _____. (neutral)

| unpleasant |
| exciting |
| horrible |

14. Monica is _____. (neutral)

15. Monica is _____. (positive)

16. Monica is _____. (negative)

| old |
| over the hill |
| mature |

Language: Usage and Practice 7, SV 1419027840

Name _____ Date _____

Idioms

> • An **idiom** is an expression that has a meaning different from the usual meanings of the individual words within it.
>   EXAMPLE: <u>Lit a fire under me</u> means "got me going," not "burned me."

 Underline the idiom in each sentence. Then write what the idiom means.

1. Jake and Ella knew they were in hot water when their car died.

   _____

2. They were miles from any town, and Ella was beside herself.

   _____

3. Jake said they should put their heads together and find a solution.

   _____

4. Ella told Jake that if he had any ideas, she was all ears.

   _____

5. Jake told her it was too soon to throw in the towel.

   _____

 Underline each idiom. Then write one definition that tells the exact meaning of the phrase and another definition that tells what the phrase means in the sentence.

6. When I finish the test, I'm going to hit the road.

   _____

   _____

7. I had to eat crow when I found out I was wrong about the test date.

   _____

   _____

8. With final exams coming, I'll have to burn the midnight oil.

   _____

   _____

9. I thought I was so smart, but the test really cut me down to size.

   _____

   _____

Language: Usage and Practice 7, SV 1419027840

Name _____   Date _____

Unit 1 Test

Choose whether the underlined words in each sentence are synonyms, antonyms, homonyms, or homographs. Darken the circle by your choice.

1. Her office is <u>up</u> the stairs and <u>down</u> the hall on the left.

   Ⓐ synonyms   Ⓑ antonyms   Ⓒ homonyms   Ⓓ homographs

2. Let's sit <u>here</u> so that we can <u>hear</u> the music well.

   Ⓐ synonyms   Ⓑ antonyms   Ⓒ homonyms   Ⓓ homographs

3. As I <u>looked</u> over my shoulder, I <u>saw</u> lightning strike a tree.

   Ⓐ synonyms   Ⓑ antonyms   Ⓒ homonyms   Ⓓ homographs

4. We saw a <u>fan</u> using a <u>fan</u> to stay cool at the baseball game.

   Ⓐ synonyms   Ⓑ antonyms   Ⓒ homonyms   Ⓓ homographs

5. He uses his left hand to throw and his <u>right</u> hand to <u>write</u>.

   Ⓐ synonyms   Ⓑ antonyms   Ⓒ homonyms   Ⓓ homographs

6. Her <u>error</u> was more than a simple <u>mistake</u>.

   Ⓐ synonyms   Ⓑ antonyms   Ⓒ homonyms   Ⓓ homographs

7. Nobody believed the man's <u>account</u> of where he got the money in his <u>account</u>.

   Ⓐ synonyms   Ⓑ antonyms   Ⓒ homonyms   Ⓓ homographs

8. Erica <u>found</u> the book her sister thought she had <u>lost</u>.

   Ⓐ synonyms   Ⓑ antonyms   Ⓒ homonyms   Ⓓ homographs

Add a prefix or suffix to the underlined word to make a new word that makes sense in the sentence. Darken the circle by your choice.

9. Hard work and luck can make you <u>fame</u>.

   Ⓐ ist   Ⓒ ous
   Ⓑ ward   Ⓓ re

10. Only criminals <u>port</u> illegal drugs.

    Ⓐ mis   Ⓒ able
    Ⓑ trans   Ⓓ re

11. People who think of others are <u>self</u>.

    Ⓐ less   Ⓒ ous
    Ⓑ ish   Ⓓ un

12. Do you <u>see</u> any problems with this?

    Ⓐ pre   Ⓒ with
    Ⓑ able   Ⓓ fore

13. You will need <u>depend</u> transportation.

    Ⓐ pre   Ⓒ ous
    Ⓑ able   Ⓓ re

14. I sometimes <u>place</u> my glasses.

    Ⓐ mis   Ⓒ ly
    Ⓑ im   Ⓓ ful

15. That is a <u>profit</u> organization.

    Ⓐ un   Ⓒ non
    Ⓑ ly   Ⓓ ous

16. The road was <u>rock</u>.

    Ⓐ ist   Ⓒ non
    Ⓑ ward   Ⓓ y

Language: Usage and Practice 7, SV 1419027840

Unit 1 Test, p. 2

Darken the circle by the correct contraction for each pair of underlined words.

17. there is

(A) ther's   (C) theres

(B) there's   (D) theres'

18. who have

(A) who've   (C) whov'e

(B) wh've   (D) who'v

19. they will

(A) the'yll   (C) they'll

(B) the'll   (D) they'll'

20. must not

(A) musn't   (C) mustnt

(B) must'nt   (D) mustn't

21. will not

(A) willn't   (C) wo'nt

(B) won't   (D) wont

22. she would

(A) shed   (C) shei'd

(B) she'ld   (D) she'd

Choose whether each underlined word has a positive connotation (+), a negative connotation (−), or is neutral (N). Darken the circle by your choice.

23. We found a scrawny dog.

(A) (+)   (B) (−)   (C) (N)

24. This book is interesting.

(A) (+)   (B) (−)   (C) (N)

25. There's a small animal.

(A) (+)   (B) (−)   (C) (N)

26. It was a foolish choice.

(A) (+)   (B) (−)   (C) (N)

27. He has a unique idea.

(A) (+)   (B) (−)   (C) (N)

28. The man had a big smile.

(A) (+)   (B) (−)   (C) (N)

29. She is not a lazy person.

(A) (+)   (B) (−)   (C) (N)

30. Please write to me sometime.

(A) (+)   (B) (−)   (C) (N)

Darken the circle by the meaning of the underlined idiom.

31. keep your chin up

(A) do less than   (C) look straight ahead
    you should

(B) accept defeat   (D) have hope

32. run across

(A) play music   (C) in a risky situation

(B) meet by chance   (D) run over

33. turn over a new leaf

(A) change your   (C) rake leaves
    ways

(B) admit   (D) be in trouble

34. beside yourself

(A) unbelievably happy (C) spend money
                            carefully

(B) very upset   (D) standing close

35. all ears

(A) listening carefully (C) having large ears

(B) meeting by chance   (D) thinking about

36. talk turkey

(A) discuss a   (C) come through
    special meal

(B) stand up for   (D) speak frankly

Recognizing Sentences

> • A **sentence** is a group of words that expresses a complete thought.
> EXAMPLE: We found a deserted cabin at the top of the hill.

❋ **Some of the following groups of words are sentences, and some are not. Write S before each group that is a sentence. Punctuate each sentence with a period.**

_____ 1. Carlos did not go to the auto show ____

_____ 2. By the side of the babbling brook ____

_____ 3. I went to the new museum last week ____

_____ 4. Mile after mile along the great highway ____

_____ 5. Check all work carefully ____

_____ 6. Down the narrow aisle of the church ____

_____ 7. I have lost my hat ____

_____ 8. On our way to work this morning ____

_____ 9. Leontyne Price, a famous singer ____

_____ 10. We saw Katherine and Sheryl yesterday ____

_____ 11. The severe cold of last winter ____

_____ 12. Once upon a time, long, long ago ____

_____ 13. There was a gorgeous sunset last night ____

_____ 14. He ran home ____

_____ 15. My brother and my sister ____

_____ 16. Mitch and Matt did a great job ____

_____ 17. We saw a beaver in the deep ravine ____

_____ 18. The cat in our neighbor's yard ____

_____ 19. Every year at the state fair ____

_____ 20. As we came to the sharp curve in the road ____

_____ 21. Just before we were ready ____

_____ 22. I heard that you and Lorenzo have a new paper route ____

_____ 23. Longfellow is called the children's poet ____

_____ 24. Into the parking garage ____

_____ 25. We washed and waxed the truck ____

_____ 26. Through the door and up the stairs ____

_____ 27. As quickly as possible ____

_____ 28. We saw the new killer whale at the zoo ____

_____ 29. Jason parked the car on the street ____

_____ 30. We had ice cream and fruit for dessert ____

Types of Sentences

- A **declarative sentence** makes a statement. It is followed by a period (.).
  - EXAMPLE: Allison is my cousin.
- An **interrogative sentence** asks a question. It is followed by a question mark (?).
  - EXAMPLE: Where was she going?
- An **imperative sentence** expresses a command or request. It is followed by a period (.).
  - EXAMPLE: Close the door.
- An **exclamatory sentence** expresses strong emotion. It can also express a command or request that is made with great excitement. It is followed by an **exclamation mark** (!).
  - EXAMPLES:
    - How you frightened me!
    - Look at that accident!

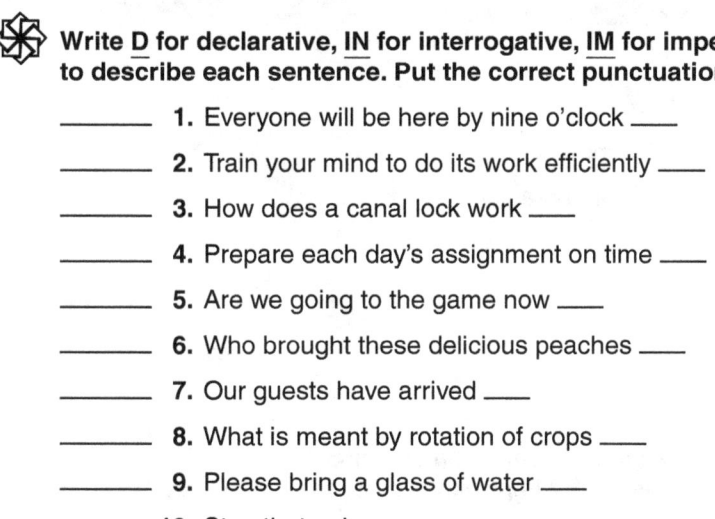 **Write D for declarative, IN for interrogative, IM for imperative, or E for exclamatory to describe each sentence. Put the correct punctuation at the end of each sentence.**

_____ **1.** Everyone will be here by nine o'clock ____

_____ **2.** Train your mind to do its work efficiently ____

_____ **3.** How does a canal lock work ____

_____ **4.** Prepare each day's assignment on time ____

_____ **5.** Are we going to the game now ____

_____ **6.** Who brought these delicious peaches ____

_____ **7.** Our guests have arrived ____

_____ **8.** What is meant by rotation of crops ____

_____ **9.** Please bring a glass of water ____

_____ **10.** Stop that noise ____

_____ **11.** Always stand erect ____

_____ **12.** Who arranged these flowers ____

_____ **13.** Anna, what do you have in that box ____

_____ **14.** The Vikings were famous sailors ____

_____ **15.** Have you solved all the problems in our lesson ____

_____ **16.** Allen, hand me that wrench ____

_____ **17.** What is the capital of California ____

_____ **18.** Cultivate a pleasant manner ____

_____ **19.** How is a pizza made ____

_____ **20.** Block that kick ____

_____ **21.** A nation is measured by the character of its people ____

_____ **22.** Are you an early riser ____

_____ **23.** Practice good table manners ____

Language: Usage and Practice 7, SV 1419027840

Types of Sentences, p. 2

✳ Write **D** for declarative, **IN** for interrogative, **IM** for imperative, or **E** for exclamatory to describe each sentence. Put the correct punctuation at the end of each sentence.

_____ **24.** What a wonderful time we've had ____

_____ **25.** How did you get here so early ____

_____ **26.** Look out for those cars ____

_____ **27.** Take good care of my dog ____

_____ **28.** There are many cotton mills in our state ____

_____ **29.** Name the capital of Nevada ____

_____ **30.** Hurrah, the game is over ____

_____ **31.** Draw a map of South America ____

_____ **32.** Geysers were first discovered in Iceland ____

_____ **33.** Have you ever been on a roller coaster ____

_____ **34.** Sweep the front walk ____

_____ **35.** Do not measure people by what they have ____

_____ **36.** A great nation is made only by worthy citizens ____

_____ **37.** Anna Moffo has sung with many of the major opera companies ____

_____ **38.** What is the longest river in the country ____

_____ **39.** Oh, you have a new car ____

_____ **40.** Andrea, why weren't you at the meeting ____

_____ **41.** Chris, I have a long piece of twine ____

_____ **42.** Paul, jump quickly ____

✳ Only one group of words in each pair below is a sentence. Circle the sentence and tell what kind it is. Write **D** for declarative, **IN** for interrogative, **IM** for imperative, or **E** for exclamatory.

_____ **43.** When will the train arrive? Two hours late.

_____ **44.** It is delayed by bad weather. Not here yet.

_____ **45.** From California. Juan and Shelly are on it.

_____ **46.** I haven't seen them in two years! Am waiting patiently.

_____ **47.** Enjoy traveling. They will stay with us for two weeks.

_____ **48.** We have many things planned for them. A good visit.

_____ **49.** They will sleep in the guest room. To our city's new zoo?

_____ **50.** Juan used to work at a zoo. Many animals.

_____ **51.** Go in the reptile house. Took care of the elephants.

_____ **52.** Each elephant had a name. Wally, Willy, and Walt.

_____ **53.** The elephants liked to train with Juan. Good job.

_____ **54.** Sandra, the elephant, had a baby. In the zoo.

_____ **55.** Male elephant. What did the zoo officials name the baby?

_____ **56.** People in the zoo. They surprised Juan!

Complete Subjects and Predicates

- Every sentence has two main parts, a **complete subject** and a **complete predicate.**
- The complete subject includes all the words that tell who or what the sentence is about.
    EXAMPLE: **All chickadees** / hunt insect eggs.
- The complete predicate includes all the words that state the action or condition of the subject.
    EXAMPLE: All chickadees / **hunt insect eggs.**

 Draw a line between the complete subject and the complete predicate in each sentence below.

1. Amy / built a bird feeder for the backyard.
2. This cleaner will remove paint.
3. Many beautiful waltzes were composed by Johann Strauss.
4. Queen Victoria ruled England for many years.
5. Eighty people are waiting in line for tickets.
6. Mario's last visit was during the summer.
7. The rocket was soon in orbit.
8. Our last meeting was held in my living room.
9. The farmers are harvesting their wheat.
10. Our new house has six rooms.
11. The heart pumps blood throughout the body.
12. This computer will help you work faster.
13. My friend has moved to Santa Fe, New Mexico.
14. A deep silence fell upon the crowd.
15. The police officers were stopping the speeding motorists.
16. The French chef prepared excellent food.
17. My father is a mechanic.
18. Antonio Salazar is running for the city council.
19. Lightning struck a tree in our yard.
20. Magazines about bicycling are becoming increasingly popular.
21. They answered every question honestly during the interview.
22. The gray twilight came before the program ended.
23. William has a way with words.
24. That section of the country has many pine forests.
25. We will have a party for Teresa on Friday.
26. Butterflies flew around the flowers.
27. The heavy bus was stuck in the mud.

Complete Subjects and Predicates, p. 2

✳ Write a sentence by adding a complete predicate to each complete subject.

28. All of the students _____.

29. Elephants _____.

30. The top of the mountain _____.

31. The television programs tonight _____.

32. I _____.

33. Each of the girls _____.

34. My father's truck _____.

35. The dam across the river _____.

36. Our new station wagon _____.

37. You _____.

38. The books in our bookcase _____.

39. The mountains _____.

40. Today's paper _____.

41. The magazine staff _____.

✳ Write a sentence by adding a complete subject to each complete predicate.

42. _____ is the largest city in Mexico.

43. _____ came to our program.

44. _____ is a valuable mineral.

45. _____ grow beside the road.

46. _____ traveled day and night.

47. _____ was a great inventor.

48. _____ wrote the letter of complaint.

49. _____ met us at the airport.

50. _____ made ice cream for the picnic.

51. _____ made a nest in our tree.

52. _____ lives near the shopping center.

53. _____ have a meeting on Saturday.

Language: Usage and Practice 7, SV 1419027840

Name _____ Date _____

Simple Subjects and Predicates

- The **simple subject** of a sentence is the main word in the complete subject.
- The simple subject is a noun or a pronoun.
- Sometimes the simple subject is also the complete subject.
    EXAMPLES:
        Our **car** / swayed in the strong wind.   **Cars** / sway in the strong wind.

 Draw a line between the complete subject and the complete predicate in each sentence below. Then underline the simple subject.

1. The plants sprouted quickly after the first rain.
2. The television program was very informative.
3. I used a word processor to write the paper.
4. My friend's truck is parked in the driveway.
5. The beavers created a dam in the river.
6. The books lined the shelves like toy soldiers.
7. Hail pounded against the storm door.
8. I bought a new mountain bike.
9. My favorite subject is history.
10. The colorful bird sang a beautiful melody.
11. The tree trunk was about five feet in diameter.
12. The sidewalk had cracks in the pavement.

- The **simple predicate** of a sentence is a verb within the complete predicate.
- The simple predicate may be made up of one word or more than one word.
    EXAMPLES:
        Our car / **swayed.**   The wind / **was blowing** hard.

 In each sentence below, draw a line between the complete subject and the complete predicate. Underline the simple predicate twice.

13. A rare Chinese vase was on display.
14. Many of the children had played.
15. All of the group went on a hike.
16. He drove the bus slowly over the slippery pavement.
17. A large number of water-skiers were on the lake last Saturday.
18. Birds have good eyesight.
19. Who discovered the Pacific Ocean?
20. I am reading the assignment now.
21. The glare of the headlights blinded us.
22. The problem on the next page is harder.

Language: Usage and Practice 7, SV 1419027840

Position of Subjects

- When the subject of a sentence comes before the verb, the sentence is in **natural order.**
    - EXAMPLE: Maria <u>went</u> home.
- When the verb or part of the verb comes before the subject, the sentence is in **inverted order.**
    - EXAMPLES:
        - On the branch <u>were</u> two <u>birds</u>.
        - There <u>are</u> four <u>children</u> in my family.
        - Here <u>is</u> my <u>friend</u>.
- Many questions are in inverted order.
    - EXAMPLE: Where <u>is</u> <u>Jim</u>?
- Sometimes the subject of a sentence is not expressed, as in a command or request. The understood subject is <u>you</u>.
    - EXAMPLE:
        - <u>Bring</u> the sandwiches.
        - (<u>You</u>) <u>bring</u> the sandwiches.

 Rewrite each inverted sentence in natural order. Rewrite commands or requests by including <u>you</u> as the subject. Then underline each simple subject once and each simple predicate twice in each sentence you write.

1. Where was the sunken treasure ship?

The sunken treasure <u>ship</u> <u>was</u> where?

2. Beyond the bridge were several sailboats.

_____

3. There is no one in that room.

_____

4. From the gymnasium came the shouts of the victorious team.

_____

5. Beside the walk grew beautiful flowers.

_____

6. When is the surprise party?

_____

7. Bring your sales report to the meeting.

_____

8. There were only three floats in the parade.

_____

9. From the yard came the bark of a dog.

_____

10. Place the forks to the left of the plate.

_____

Language: Usage and Practice 7, SV 1419027840

Name _____ Date _____

Compound Subjects

> • A **compound subject** is made up of two or more simple subjects.
>   EXAMPLE: **Leon** and **Tanya** / are tall people.

✳ **Draw a line between the complete subject and the complete predicate in each sentence.
Write SS on the line for a simple subject. Write CS for a compound subject.**

___CS___ 1. Arturo and I / often work late on Friday.

_____ 2. Sandy left the person near the crowded exit.

_____ 3. She and I will mail the packages to San Francisco, California, today.

_____ 4. Shanghai and New Delhi were two cities visited by the group.

_____ 5. The fire spread rapidly to other buildings in the neighborhood.

_____ 6. Luis and Lenora helped their parents with the chores.

_____ 7. Swimming, jogging, and hiking were our favorite sports.

_____ 8. Melbourne and Sydney are important Australian cities.

_____ 9. Eric and I had an interesting experience Saturday.

_____ 10. The Red Sea and the Mediterranean Sea are connected by the Suez Canal.

_____ 11. The Republicans and the Democrats made many speeches before the election.

_____ 12. The people waved to us from the top of the cliff.

_____ 13. Liz and Jim crated the freshly picked apples.

_____ 14. Clean clothes and a neat appearance are important in an interview.

_____ 15. The kitten and the old dog are good friends.

_____ 16. Jason and Justin are on their way to the swimming pool.

_____ 17. Tom combed his dog's shiny black coat.

_____ 18. Redbud and dogwood trees bloom in the spring.

_____ 19. I hummed a cheerful tune on the way to the meeting.

_____ 20. Buffalo, deer, and antelope once roamed the plains of North America.

_____ 21. Gina and Hiroshi raked the leaves.

_____ 22. New Orleans and Baton Rouge are two cities in Louisiana.

_____ 23. Hang gliding is a popular sport in Hawaii.

_____ 24. Our class went on a field trip to the aquarium.

_____ 25. The doctor asked him to get a blood test.

✳ **Write two sentences containing compound subjects.**

26. _____

27. _____

Language: Usage and Practice 7, SV 1419027840

Compound Predicates

> • A **compound predicate** is made up of two or more simple predicates.
>   EXAMPLE: Little Jaz / **dances** and **sings.**

✳ **Draw a line between the complete subject and the complete predicate in each sentence. Write <u>SP</u> on the line for each simple predicate. Write <u>CP</u> for each compound predicate.**

_____ 1. Edward grinned and nodded.

_____ 2. Plants need air to live.

_____ 3. Old silver teakettles were among their possessions.

_____ 4. My sister buys and sells real estate.

_____ 5. Snow covered every highway in the area.

_____ 6. Mr. Sanders designs and makes odd pieces of furniture.

_____ 7. Popcorn is one of my favorite snack foods.

_____ 8. Soccer is one of my favorite sports.

_____ 9. The ducks quickly crossed the road and found the ducklings.

_____ 10. They came early and stayed late.

_____ 11. Crystal participated in the Special Olympics this year.

_____ 12. Josie raked and sacked the leaves.

_____ 13. Perry built the fire and cooked supper.

_____ 14. We collected old newspapers for the recycling center.

_____ 15. Doug arrived in Toronto, Ontario, during the afternoon.

_____ 16. Tony's parents are visiting in Oregon and Washington.

_____ 17. The Herreras live in that two-story house on Oak Street.

_____ 18. The shingles were picked up and delivered today.

_____ 19. The audience talked and laughed before the performance.

_____ 20. Automobiles crowd and jam that highway early in the morning.

_____ 21. The apples and pears are rotting in the boxes.

_____ 22. The leader of the group grumbled and scolded.

_____ 23. She worked hard and waited patiently.

_____ 24. Ichiro collects old black-and-white photographs.

_____ 25. The supervisor has completed the work for the week.

✳ **Write two sentences containing compound predicates.**

26. _____

27. _____

Combining Sentences

- Two sentences in which the subjects are different and the predicates are the same can be combined into one sentence.
- The two subjects are joined by <u>and</u>.
    EXAMPLE:
    Hurricanes are storms.
    Tornadoes are storms.
    Hurricanes and tornadoes are storms.
- Two sentences in which the subjects are the same and the predicates are different can be combined into one sentence.
- The two predicates may be joined by <u>or</u>, <u>and</u>, or <u>but</u>.
    EXAMPLE:
    Hurricanes **begin over tropical oceans.**
    Hurricanes **move inland.**
    Hurricanes **begin over tropical oceans and move inland.**

 Combine each pair of sentences below. Underline the compound subject or the compound predicate in each sentence that you write.

1. Lightning is part of a thunderstorm. Thunder is part of a thunderstorm.

_____

2. Thunderstorms usually happen in the spring. Thunderstorms bring heavy rains.

_____

3. Depending on how close or far away it is, thunder sounds like a sharp crack.
Depending on how close or far away it is, thunder rumbles.

_____

_____

4. Lightning is very exciting to watch. Lightning can be very dangerous.

_____

5. Lightning causes many fires. Lightning harms many people.

_____

6. An open field is an unsafe place to be during a thunderstorm.
A golf course is an unsafe place to be during a thunderstorm.

_____

_____

7. Benjamin Franklin wanted to protect people from lightning.
Benjamin Franklin invented the lightning rod.

_____

_____

8. A lightning rod is a metal rod placed on the top of a building.
A lightning rod is connected to the ground by a cable.

_____

_____

Direct Objects

> • The **direct object** tells who or what receives the action of the verb.
> • The direct object is a noun or pronoun that follows an action verb.
>
> DO
> EXAMPLE: You told the **truth.**

 Underline the verb in each sentence. Then write DO above each direct object.

1. Elephants can carry logs with their trunks.

2. Who made this magazine rack?

3. Do you always plan a daily schedule?

4. They easily won the game.

5. Mama baked an apple pie for dinner.

6. Who tuned your piano?

7. I take guitar lessons once a week.

8. Who composed this melody?

9. I especially enjoy mystery stories.

10. The astronauts orbited the moon several times.

11. I bought this coat in New York.

12. Did he find his glasses?

13. Anne drove the truck to the hardware store.

14. The boy shrugged his shoulders.

15. We have finished our work today.

16. We drink milk with breakfast.

17. She can solve any problem quickly.

18. Who made our first flag?

19. You will learn something from this lesson.

20. Every person needs friends.

21. I have found a dime.

22. Yuko ate an apple for a snack.

Indirect Objects

- The **indirect object** is the noun or pronoun that tells to whom or for whom an action is done.
- To have an indirect object, a sentence must have a direct object.
- The indirect object is usually placed between the action verb and the direct object.

                IO   DO

  EXAMPLE: Who sold **you** that fantastic **bike**?

 Underline the verb in each sentence. Then write DO above the direct object and IO above the indirect object.

1. Certain marine plants give the Red Sea its color.

2. I gave the cashier a check for twenty dollars.

3. The magician showed the audience a few of her tricks.

4. The coach taught them the rules of the game.

5. Roberto brought us some foreign coins.

6. This interesting book will give every reader pleasure.

7. Have you written your brother a letter?

8. They made us some sandwiches to take on our hike.

9. The astronaut gave Mission Control the data.

10. I bought my friend an etching at the art exhibit.

11. Jim, did you sell Mike your old car?

12. We have given the dog a thorough scrubbing.

13. Give the usher your ticket.

14. Carlo brought my brother a gold ring from Mexico.

15. Hand me a pencil, please.

16. The conductor gave the orchestra a short break.

17. Show me the picture of your boat.

18. I have given you my money.

19. Give Leeza this message.

20. The club gave the town a new statue.

Independent and Subordinate Clauses

> - A **clause** is a group of words that contains a subject and a predicate.
> - There are two kinds of clauses: **independent clauses** and **subordinate clauses.**
> - An **independent clause** can stand alone as a sentence because it expresses a complete thought.
>   EXAMPLE:
>   **The students came in** when the bell rang.
>   **The students came in.**

 Underline the independent clause in each sentence below.

1. Frank will be busy because he is studying.

2. I have only one hour that I can spare.

3. The project must be finished when I get back.

4. Gloria volunteered to do the typing that needs to be done.

5. The work is going too slowly for us to finish on time.

6. Before Nathan started to help, I didn't think we could finish.

7. What else should we do before we relax?

8. Since you forgot to give this page to Gloria, you can type it.

9. After she had finished typing, we completed the project.

10. We actually got it finished before the deadline.

> - A **subordinate clause** has a subject and predicate but cannot stand alone as a sentence because it does not express a complete thought.
> - A subordinate clause must be combined with an independent clause to make a sentence.
>   EXAMPLE: The stamp **that I bought** was already in my collection.

 Underline the subordinate clause in each sentence below.

11. The people who went shopping found a great sale.

12. Tony's bike, which is a mountain bike, came from that store.

13. Juana was sad when the sale was over.

14. Miriam was excited because she wanted some new things.

15. Ron didn't find anything since he went late.

16. The mall where we went shopping was new.

17. The people who own the stores are proud of the beautiful setting.

18. The mall, which is miles away, is serviced by the city bus.

19. We ran as fast as we could because the bus was coming.

20. We were panting because we had run fast.

Adjective Clauses

> - An **adjective clause** is a subordinate clause that modifies a noun or a pronoun.
> - It answers the adjective question <u>Which one?</u> or <u>What kind?</u> It usually modifies the word directly preceding it.
> - Most adjective clauses begin with a **relative pronoun**. A relative pronoun relates an adjective clause to the noun or pronoun that the clause modifies.
> - <u>Who</u>, <u>whose</u>, <u>which</u>, and <u>that</u> are relative pronouns.
>   EXAMPLE: The coat **that I bought** was on sale.
>   ꜜꜜꜜꜜꜜ noun   adjective clause

 Underline the adjective clause in each sentence below.

1. A compass has a needle that always points northward.

2. A seismograph is an instrument that measures earthquake tremors.

3. People who work in science laboratories today have a broad field of study.

4. This will be the first time that she has played in that position.

5. Jay is the person whose wrist was broken.

6. The fish that I caught was large.

7. A sentence that contains a subordinate clause is a complex sentence.

8. Here is the photograph that I promised to show you.

9. The book that I read was very humorous.

 Add an adjective clause to each independent clause below.

10. A microscope is an instrument (that) _____
_____

11. Amelia Earhart was a pilot (who) _____
_____

12. We have football players (who) _____
_____

13. They built a helicopter (that) _____
_____

14. Bunny is a cat (that) _____
_____

15. A telescope is an instrument (that) _____
_____

Name _____ Date _____

Adverb Clauses

- An **adverb clause** is a subordinate clause that modifies a verb, an adjective, or another adverb.
- It answers the adverb question <u>How?</u>, <u>Under what condition?</u>, or <u>Why?</u>
- Words that introduce adverb clauses are called **subordinating conjunctions**.
- The many subordinating conjunctions include such words as <u>when</u>, <u>after</u>, <u>before</u>, <u>since</u>, <u>although</u>, and <u>because</u>.
  EXAMPLE: I finished **before the bell rang**.
  adverb clause

 Underline the adverb clause in each sentence below.

1. We had agreed to go hiking when the cloudy skies cleared.

2. Although the weather was mild and sunny, we took along our jackets.

3. Clouds began to move in once again after we arrived at the park.

4. We felt comfortable about the weather because we were prepared.

5. Since we had our jackets, we didn't get too cold.

6. Although the clouds remained, it never rained.

7. It was exhilarating to see the view when we got to the top of the hill.

8. After enjoying the beauty and the quiet for a while, we hiked back down.

9. We decided to drive home the long way since it was still early.

10. We had a wonderful day because we were so relaxed and happy.

 Add an adverb clause to each independent clause below.

11. We ate breakfast (before) _____

_____

12. Jason and I carried umbrellas (since) _____

_____

13. We took the bus to the museum (because) _____

_____

14. People in line waited (when) _____

_____

15. We saw the exhibit (after) _____

_____

16. Latrelle and I baked cookies (when) _____

_____

Language: Usage and Practice 7, SV 1419027840

Name _____   Date _____

Simple and Compound Sentences

- A **simple sentence** contains only one independent clause. The subject, the predicate, or both may be compound.
    - EXAMPLES:
        The courthouse / is the oldest building in town.
        Gale and Louisa / are making costumes and dressing up.
- A **compound sentence** consists of two or more independent clauses.
- Each independent clause in a compound sentence can stand alone as a separate sentence.
- The independent clauses are usually joined by <u>and</u>, <u>but</u>, <u>so</u>, <u>or</u>, <u>for</u>, or <u>yet</u> and a comma.
    - EXAMPLE: Jackson brought the chairs, but Maryanne forgot the extra table.
- Sometimes a **semicolon (;)** is used to join two independent clauses in a compound sentence.
    - EXAMPLE: The music started; the dance had begun.

 Write S before each simple sentence, and write CS before each compound sentence.

_____ **1.** We can wait for Janna, or we can go on ahead.

_____ **2.** The carnival will start today in the empty lot.

_____ **3.** Justo and Manuel are going to meet us there at six o'clock.

_____ **4.** I really want to go to the carnival, yet I am not sure about going tonight.

_____ **5.** I didn't mean to hurt Carlene's feelings by not going.

_____ **6.** You wait for the package, and I'll meet you at the carnival.

_____ **7.** I can't skip my homework to go, but maybe I'll finish it this afternoon.

_____ **8.** Jan and Alicia are both working at the carnival this year.

Put brackets ([ ]) around the independent clauses in each compound sentence. Then underline the word or punctuation used to join the clauses.

9. You must observe all the rules, or you must withdraw from the race.

10. I did well on the test, and Maria did well, too.

11. Shall I carry this box, or do you want to leave it here?

12. We must closely guard our freedom, or an enemy will take it from us.

13. He threw a beautiful pass, but no one caught it.

14. The doctor treated the cut, but he did not have to make any stitches.

15. I like to spend weekends at home, but the others prefer to travel.

16. The year is almost over, and everyone is thinking of the new year.

17. The family faced every hardship, yet they were thankful for what they had.

18. Move the box over here; I'll unpack it.

19. Candace likes football; Jarrett prefers soccer.

20. I drive safely, and I always make everyone fasten seat belts.

21. Please get the telephone number, and I'll call after work.

Complex Sentences

- A **complex sentence** contains one independent clause and one or more subordinate clauses.

  EXAMPLE: The person **who helps me carry these packages** will get some dessert.   subordinate clause

 Put brackets around the subordinate clause and underline the independent clause in each complex sentence below.

1. The shadows [that had fallen between the trees] were a deep purple.

2. The soldiers waded across the stream where the water was shallow.

3. They waited for me until the last bus came.

4. The fans of that team were sad when the team lost the game.

5. When George was here, he was charmed by the beauty of the hills.

6. Sophia will call for you when she is ready.

7. Some spiders that are found in Sumatra have legs seventeen inches long.

8. Those who are going will arrive on time.

9. Do not throw the bat after you've hit the ball.

10. Tell us about the trip that you made a year ago.

 Add a subordinate clause that begins with the word in parentheses to make a complex sentence.

11. I try not to drive (where) _____

_____

12. The electric light is an important invention (that) _____

_____

13. The telephone stopped ringing (before) _____

_____

14. He is the man (who) _____

_____

15. This is the book (that) _____

_____

16. Turn to the left (when) _____

_____

Language: Usage and Practice 7, SV 1419027840

Correcting Run-on Sentences

- Two or more independent clauses that are run together without the correct punctuation are called a **run-on sentence**.
    EXAMPLE: The music was deafening, I turned down the volume.
- One way to correct a run-on sentence is to separate it into two sentences.
    EXAMPLE: The music was deafening. I turned down the volume.
- Another way to correct a run-on sentence is to make it into a compound sentence.
    EXAMPLE: The music was deafening, so I turned down the volume.
- Another way to correct a run-on sentence is to use a semicolon.
    EXAMPLE: The music was deafening; I turned down the volume.

 Correct each run-on sentence below by writing it as two sentences or as a compound sentence.

1. The city council held a meeting a meeting is held every month.

_____

_____

2. The council members are elected by the voters there are two thousand voters in the city.

_____

_____

3. There is one council member from each suburb, the president is elected by the council members.

_____

_____

4. Those who run for office must give speeches, the speeches should be short.

_____

_____

5. The council decides on many activities every activity is voted on.

_____

_____

6. Money is needed for many of the special activities, the council also plans fund-raisers in the city.

_____

_____

7. The annual city picnic is sponsored by the city council the picnic is in May.

_____

_____

Language: Usage and Practice 7, SV 1419027840

Name _____ Date _____

Expanding Sentences

- Sentences can be **expanded** by adding details to make them clearer and more interesting.
  EXAMPLE:
  The audience laughed.
  The **excited** audience **in the theater** laughed **loudly.**
- Details added to sentences may answer these questions: When? Where? How? How often? To what degree? What kind? Which? How many?

 Expand each sentence below by adding details to answer the questions shown in parentheses. Write the expanded sentence on the line.

1. The car stalled. (What kind? Where?)

   _____

2. Marvin raised the hood. (How? Which?)

   _____

3. Smoke billowed from the engine. (What kind? Where?)

   _____

4. He called the service station. (When? Which?)

   _____

5. The phone rang. (Which? How often?)

   _____

Decide how each of the following sentences can be expanded. Write your expanded sentence on the line.

6. The runner crossed the finish line.

   _____

7. The crowd cheered.

   _____

8. The reporter interviewed her.

   _____

9. She answered.

   _____

10. Her coach ran up to her.

    _____

11. She and her coach walked off the track.

    _____

12. She was awarded the medal.

    _____

Name _____ Date _____

Unit 2 Test

Darken the circle by the type that names each sentence.

1. Please answer the front door. Ⓐ declarative Ⓑ interrogative Ⓒ imperative Ⓓ exclamatory

2. Who's at the door? Ⓐ declarative Ⓑ interrogative Ⓒ imperative Ⓓ exclamatory

3. It's your friend Jesse. Ⓐ declarative Ⓑ interrogative Ⓒ imperative Ⓓ exclamatory

4. I can't believe it! Ⓐ declarative Ⓑ interrogative Ⓒ imperative Ⓓ exclamatory

Darken the circle by the correct end punctuation for each sentence.

5. You scared me to death Ⓐ . Ⓑ ? Ⓒ !

6. Why are you doing that Ⓐ . Ⓑ ? Ⓒ !

7. Please get some more ice Ⓐ . Ⓑ ? Ⓒ !

8. I think it's going to rain Ⓐ . Ⓑ ? Ⓒ !

Darken the circle by the sentences that have a line drawn between the complete subject and the complete predicate.

9. Ⓐ Jeanne writes / me every month.
   Ⓑ The newspaper told all / about the council meeting.
   Ⓒ Dana's cousin and his friend / are visiting for the week.
   Ⓓ It snowed / for the first time all winter.

10. Ⓐ The longest day / of the year is in June.
    Ⓑ Most of the people stood / in line for hours.
    Ⓒ All of the guests / enjoyed the party.
    Ⓓ Joe and Ming will be / leaving soon.

Darken the circle by the sentences in which the simple subject is underlined.

11. Ⓐ <u>Their</u> house is for sale.
    Ⓑ <u>That</u> is a great story.
    Ⓒ Our <u>neighbors</u> are very friendly.
    Ⓓ That store has many <u>kinds</u> of costumes.

12. Ⓐ The <u>first thing</u> to do is remove the cover.
    Ⓑ <u>Her</u> jacket was torn.
    Ⓒ The fresh <u>bread</u> smelled wonderful.
    Ⓓ The answer to the <u>question</u> was wrong.

Darken the circle by the sentence in which the simple predicate is underlined.

13. Ⓐ Caroline <u>had heard</u> them at the concert.
    Ⓑ I <u>can</u> remember everyone who went.
    Ⓒ Pablo <u>has been</u> practicing all morning.
    Ⓓ <u>Jennifer</u> brought some fresh vegetables.

Darken the circle by the sentence that is written in natural order.

14. Ⓐ Always this trip I will remember.
    Ⓑ Around the corner is the drugstore.
    Ⓒ The lights suddenly went out.
    Ⓓ Did you turn off the oven?

Unit 2 Test, p. 2

Darken the circle by the sentence that has a compound subject.

15. Ⓐ Juanita and Teo went to the movies.

    Ⓑ Pearl, Lily's dog, came home muddy.

    Ⓒ Exercise is good for your health.

    Ⓓ The horse trotted and pranced.

Darken the circle by the sentence that has a compound predicate.

16. Ⓐ The clerk totaled the check.

    Ⓑ Robert and Candace traveled to Europe.

    Ⓒ The skater jumped and spun in the air.

    Ⓓ The old oak tree split in half.

Identify each underlined word. Darken the circle by your choice.

17. We brought them some souvenirs.

    Ⓐ direct object

    Ⓑ indirect object

18. Teresa sent me postcards from Italy.

    Ⓐ direct object

    Ⓑ indirect object

Darken the circle by the type of clause underlined in each sentence.

19. We followed the crowd as it moved toward the exit.

    Ⓐ independent

    Ⓑ subordinate

20. When the music stopped, everyone clapped.

    Ⓐ independent

    Ⓑ subordinate

Darken the circle by the way the underlined subordinate clause is used in each sentence.

21. We went swimming when the weather improved.   Ⓐ adjective clause   Ⓑ adverb clause

22. The cabin that is next to ours is vacant.   Ⓐ adjective clause   Ⓑ adverb clause

Darken the circle by the correct description for each sentence.

23. Tony loves to go shopping.
    Ⓐ simple   Ⓒ complex
    Ⓑ compound   Ⓓ run-on

24. He often asks Anika to go, sometimes she does.
    Ⓐ simple   Ⓒ complex
    Ⓑ compound   Ⓓ run-on

25. They like to shop together, but Anika doesn't like to browse.
    Ⓐ simple   Ⓒ complex
    Ⓑ compound   Ⓓ run-on

26. She prefers to buy only what she's looking for when she shops.
    Ⓐ simple   Ⓒ complex
    Ⓑ compound   Ⓓ run-on

27. Tony, who loves browsing, would rather spend more time looking.
    Ⓐ simple   Ⓒ complex
    Ⓑ compound   Ⓓ run-on

28. They always agree on a plan, and then they both enjoy the outing.
    Ⓐ simple   Ⓒ complex
    Ⓑ compound   Ⓓ run-on

Nouns

> • A **noun** is a word that names a person, place, thing, or quality.
> EXAMPLE: **Natalia Nord** is my **friend.**

 Circle the nouns in each sentence.

1. Lupe Garcia has worked here for years and is now a supervisor.

2. The triangular piece of land at the mouth of a river is called a delta.

3. Gilbert Stuart, an American artist, painted the portraits of five American presidents.

4. Albert Einstein, a very famous scientist, was born in Germany.

5. The greatest library of the ancient world was in Alexandria, Egypt.

6. Jim Thorpe, born in Oklahoma, is ranked among the greatest athletes of all time.

7. Mahalia Jackson was noted as a singer of spirituals.

8. Marconi invented the wireless telegraph.

9. Do you watch the parades and football games on television on New Year's Day?

10. Terry Fox, a runner who lost a leg to cancer, ran 3,339 miles across Canada.

11. The *Boston News-Letter* was the first newspaper in the United States.

12. The first wireless message was sent across the English Channel in the nineteenth century.

13. Chicago is a city on Lake Michigan.

14. His seat is by the window.

15. Kuang likes his new car.

16. They have promised their children a trip to Carlsbad Caverns.

17. Washington, D.C., is the capital of the United States.

18. France grows more food than any other country in Western Europe.

19. Maria was excited about her new saxophone.

20. Hailstones are frozen raindrops, but snowflakes are not.

21. The nights are usually warm in the summer.

22. Many rivers were named by explorers.

23. Jeff built a carport to store his boat.

24. California is home to many movie stars.

25. William Caxton printed the first book in England.

26. Chris bought tomatoes, lettuce, and cherries at the market.

27. That building has offices, stores, and apartments.

28. Laticia drove to Peoria, Illinois, to see her friend.

29. The airport was closed for five hours due to a snowstorm.

30. My pen is almost out of ink.

Name _____ Date _____

Common and Proper Nouns

- There are two main classes of nouns: common nouns and proper nouns.
- A **common noun** names any one of a class of objects.
    EXAMPLES: child   tree   home
- A **proper noun** names a particular person, place, or thing. It begins with a capital letter.
    EXAMPLES: Ronald Reagan   Toronto   Statue of Liberty

 Underline the common nouns and circle the proper nouns in each sentence.

1. In the story, a prince and a pauper changed clothing.

2. New York and Los Angeles are the largest cities in the United States.

3. Do you remember the story about Scrooge and Tiny Tim?

4. Sumatra is a large island in the Indian Ocean.

5. In the United States, hail causes more damage than tornadoes do.

6. We learned to make paper from the Chinese.

7. "Rikki-tikki-tavi," by Rudyard Kipling, is a story about a mongoose.

8. *Shamrock* is the name commonly given to the national emblem of Ireland.

9. The shilling was a silver coin used in England.

10. The lights of our car were reflected in the wet pavement.

11. Nathan, did you come with Samuel last Tuesday?

12. The Great Sphinx is the most famous monument in Egypt.

13. My family visited Mexico and Canada this year.

 Write a common noun suggested by each proper noun.

14. Panama _____

15. *Treasure Island* _____

16. Lindsey _____

17. Kansas _____

18. Beethoven _____

19. Pacific _____

20. Iceland _____

21. Saturn _____

22. Ms. Taylor _____

23. Africa _____

24. Edison _____

25. North America _____

26. December _____

27. Toronto _____

28. University of Ottawa _____

29. Rocky Mountain _____

30. Dr. Dean _____

31. Huron _____

32. Tuesday _____

33. Thanksgiving _____

Language: Usage and Practice 7, SV 1419027840

Common and Proper Nouns, p. 2

 Write a proper noun suggested by each common noun.

34. continent _____

35. mountain _____

36. hotel _____

37. hero _____

38. inventor _____

39. building _____

40. day _____

41. physician _____

42. holiday _____

43. state _____

44. actor _____

45. magazine _____

46. month _____

47. lake _____

48. school _____

49. river _____

50. song _____

51. president _____

52. explorer _____

53. basketball team _____

 Write a sentence in which you use a proper noun suggested to you by each phrase.

54. Your state or province _____

_____

55. Name of a foreign country _____

_____

56. Name of a singer _____

_____

57. Name of the make of an automobile _____

_____

58. Name of a store near your home _____

_____

59. Name of a television star _____

_____

60. Name of an ocean _____

_____

61. Name of the President of the United States _____

_____

Language: Usage and Practice 7, SV 1419027840

Singular and Plural Nouns

The following chart shows how to change **singular nouns** into **plural nouns.**

Noun	Plural Form	Examples
Most nouns	Add s	ship, ships nose, noses
Nouns ending in a consonant and y	Change the y to i and add es	sky, skies navy, navies
Nouns ending in o	Add s or es	hero, heroes piano, pianos
Most nouns ending in f or fe	Change the f or fe to ves	half, halves
Most nouns ending in ch, sh, s, or x	Add es	bench, benches bush, bushes tax, taxes
Many two-word or three-word compound nouns	Add s to the principal word	son-in-law, sons-in-law
Nouns with the same form in the singular and plural	No change	sheep

✳ **Complete each sentence by writing the plural form of the word in parentheses.**

1. (brush)   These are plastic _____.

2. (lunch)   That cafe on the corner serves well-balanced _____.

3. (country)   What _____ belong to the United Nations?

4. (bench)   There are many iron _____ in the park.

5. (earring)   These _____ came from Italy.

6. (calf)   How many _____ are in that pen?

7. (piano)   There are three _____ in the warehouse.

8. (fox)   Did you see the _____ at the zoo?

9. (daisy)   We bought Shera a bunch of _____.

10. (potato)   Do you like baked _____?

11. (dish)   Please help wash the _____.

12. (store)   There are three _____ near my house.

Language: Usage and Practice 7, SV 1419027840

Name _____ Date _____

Singular and Plural Nouns, p. 2

 Write the correct plural form for each singular noun.

13. booklet _____

14. tomato _____

15. truck _____

16. chef _____

17. branch _____

18. toddler _____

19. penny _____

20. echo _____

21. piece _____

22. door _____

23. island _____

24. cherry _____

25. house _____

26. garage _____

27. fish _____

28. watch _____

29. elf _____

30. desk _____

31. pan _____

32. sheep _____

33. garden _____

34. pony _____

35. solo _____

36. tree _____

37. light _____

38. church _____

39. city _____

40. spoonful _____

41. vacation _____

42. home _____

 Rewrite the sentences, changing each underlined singular noun to a plural noun.

43. Put the <u>apple</u> and <u>orange</u> in the <u>box</u>.

_____

44. Jan wrote five <u>letter</u> to her <u>friend</u>.

_____

45. Those <u>building</u> each have four <u>elevator</u>.

_____

46. Our <u>family</u> drove many <u>mile</u> to get to the <u>lake</u>.

_____

47. The <u>top</u> of those <u>car</u> were damaged in the <u>storm</u>.

_____

48. My <u>aunt</u> and <u>uncle</u> attended the family reunion.

_____

Name _____ Date _____

Possessive Nouns

- A **possessive noun** shows possession of the noun that follows.
- Form the possessive of most singular nouns by adding an apostrophe (') and s̲.
  EXAMPLES: a **child's** toy   my **teacher's** classroom
- Form the possessive of plural nouns ending in s̲ by adding only an apostrophe.
  EXAMPLES: our **books'** pages   those **stores'** windows
- Form the possessive of plural nouns that do not end in s̲ by adding an apostrophe and s̲.
  EXAMPLES: some **women's** clothes   many **men's** shoes

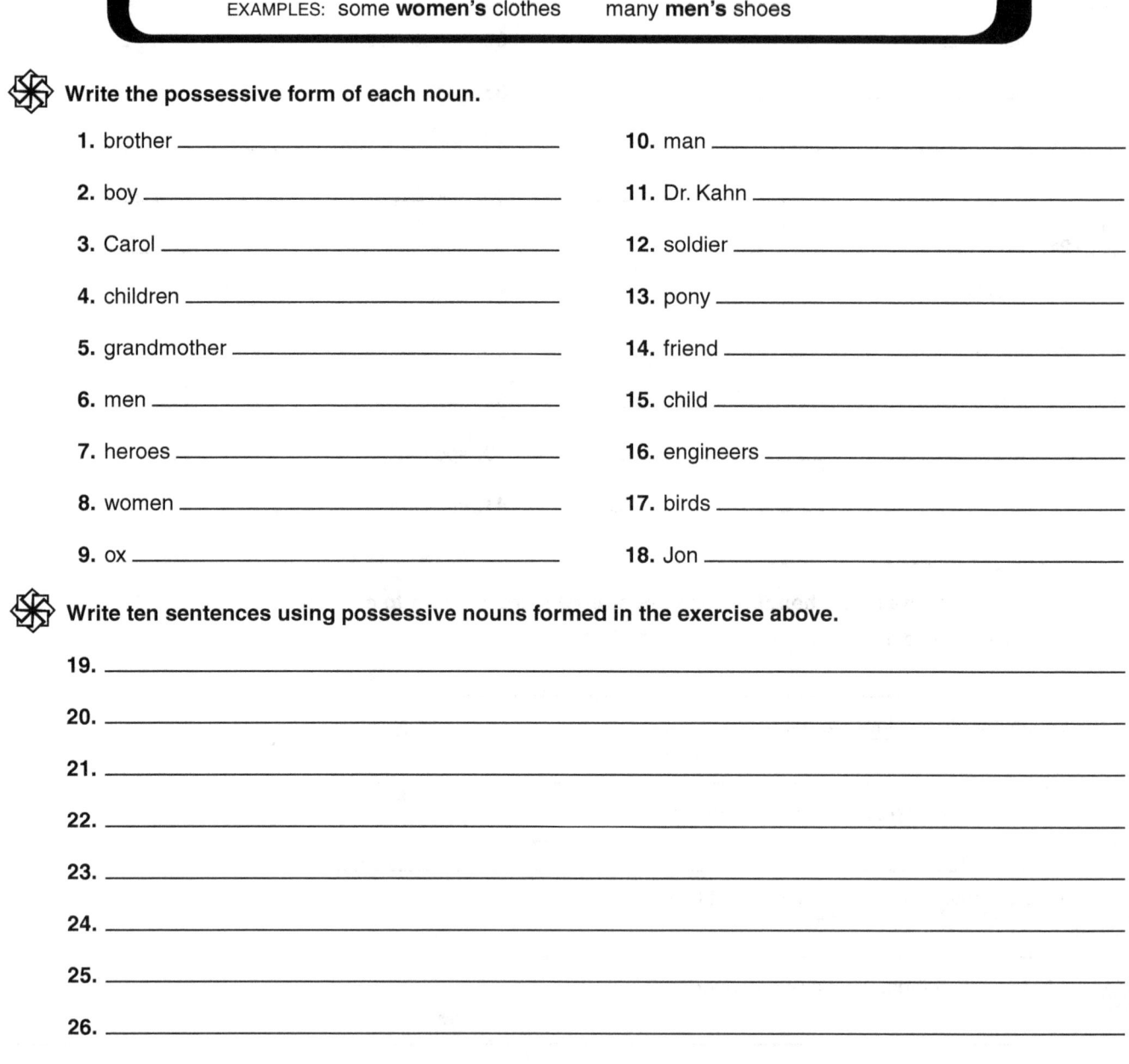

Write the possessive form of each noun.

1. brother _____

2. boy _____

3. Carol _____

4. children _____

5. grandmother _____

6. men _____

7. heroes _____

8. women _____

9. ox _____

10. man _____

11. Dr. Kahn _____

12. soldier _____

13. pony _____

14. friend _____

15. child _____

16. engineers _____

17. birds _____

18. Jon _____

Write ten sentences using possessive nouns formed in the exercise above.

19. _____

20. _____

21. _____

22. _____

23. _____

24. _____

25. _____

26. _____

27. _____

28. _____

Language: Usage and Practice 7, SV 1419027840

Name _____ Date _____

Possessive Nouns, p. 2

✳ **Complete each sentence with the possessive form of the word in parentheses.**

29. (doctor)   My _____ office is closed.

30. (senator)   The _____ speech was astounding.

31. (sheep)   What is the old saying about a wolf in _____ clothing?

32. (baby)   Are the _____ hands cold?

33. (instructor)   My _____ classroom is on this floor.

34. (collectors)   Let's form a _____ club.

35. (spider)   A _____ web has a complicated design.

36. (Mr. Takata)   _____ store was damaged by the flood.

37. (Chet)   _____ brother found this purse.

38. (Lawanda)   _____ business is successful.

39. (Carl Sandburg)   _____ poems are enjoyed by people of all ages.

40. (child)   The _____ book is torn.

41. (women)   That store sells _____ clothing.

42. (elephants)   There were seats on the _____ backs.

43. (sister)   My _____ room is at the front of the house.

44. (Brazil)   What is the name of _____ largest river?

45. (friends)   Those are my _____ homes.

46. (bird)   That _____ nest is very close to the ground.

47. (children)   The library has a table of _____ books.

48. (owl)   I heard an _____ hoot during the night.

49. (brothers)   Please get your _____ shirts from the dryer.

50. (student)   The _____ pen ran out of ink.

51. (country)   We sang our _____ national anthem.

52. (owner)   The dog lay at its _____ feet.

53. (uncle)   I visited my _____ laundry.

54. (Jolene)   _____ paintings sell well.

55. (men)   The _____ jackets are brown.

Appositives

- An **appositive** is a noun that identifies or explains the noun or pronoun it follows.
  EXAMPLE: My dog, **Fireball**, won a medal.
- An **appositive phrase** consists of an appositive and its modifiers.
  EXAMPLE: His book, **a novel about the Civil War,** is one of the best I've read.
- Use **commas** to set off an appositive or an appositive phrase that is not essential to the meaning of the sentence.
  EXAMPLE: John Gray, **my uncle,** owns that home.
- Don't use commas if the appositive is essential to the meaning of the sentence.
  EXAMPLES: My brother **Kevin** arrived late. My brother **Charlie** arrived early.

 Underline the appositive or appositive phrase and circle the noun that it identifies.

1. Banff, the large Canadian national park, is my favorite place to visit.

2. The painter Vincent Van Gogh cut off part of his ear.

3. The White House, home of the President of the United States, is open to the public for tours.

4. Uncle Marco, my mother's brother, is an engineer.

5. Earth, the only inhabited planet in our solar system, is home to a diverse population of plants and animals.

6. The scorpion, a native of the southwestern part of North America, has a poisonous sting.

7. Emily's prize Persian cat, Amelia, won first prize at the cat show.

8. Judge Andropov, the presiding judge, sentenced the criminal to prison.

9. Paula's friend from Florida, Luisa, watched a space shuttle launch.

Complete each sentence with an appropriate appositive.

10. My friend _____ bought a new bike.

11. The bike, _____, is fast and sleek.

12. Joe and his friend _____ plan to ride their bikes together.

13. They will ride to Pease Park, _____, on Saturday.

14. They plan to meet Anne, _____, on the bike path.

15. After bicycling, they will see a movie, _____.

16. Our friend _____ might come with us.

17. We will get a snack, _____, to eat during the movie.

18. My favorite actor, _____, might be in the movie.

Action Verbs

> • A **verb** is a word that expresses action, being, or state of being.
>   EXAMPLE: Paul **went** to the store.
> • An **action verb** is a verb that expresses action.
>   EXAMPLE: The track star **ran** fast.

 Underline the action verb in each sentence.

1. Watch your favorite television program.

2. Andrea carefully dusted her new piano.

3. Hanna, copy the pages carefully.

4. A wood fire burned in the huge fireplace.

5. This button fell from my sweater.

6. The Harlem Globetrotters play basketball throughout the world.

7. The musicians practiced for the concert.

8. The waves dashed the light craft against the rocks.

9. A sentence expresses a complete thought.

10. Everybody enjoys a good laugh.

11. This long, narrow trail leads to the mountaintop.

12. It snowed almost every day in February.

13. We hiked through the southern part of Arizona.

14. Sam made me a delicious sandwich.

15. Please hand me the salt, Dannette.

16. Draw a line under each verb.

17. We skated on Lake Superior.

18. The woman answered all my questions.

19. The city repaired that pothole last week.

20. Early settlers suffered many hardships.

21. Write your sentence on the board.

22. They moved the car from the street.

23. Thomas Edison often worked eighteen hours a day.

24. Angelina directs the community choir.

25. The team played softball all afternoon.

26. We walked along the beach for an hour.

27. Who helped you with your science project?

28. The bridge collapsed.

29. The antique clock ticked loudly.

Linking Verbs

> - A **linking verb** does not show action. Instead, it links the subject to a word that either describes the subject or gives the subject another name.
> - A verb is a linking verb if it can replace one of the verbs of being (<u>am</u>, <u>is</u>, <u>are</u>, <u>was</u>, <u>were</u>).
>   EXAMPLES:
>   We **were** cold.
>   Nanzy **is** a dancer.
>   Jason **looked** tired.
>   The soup **tastes** delicious.

 Underline the linking verb in each sentence.

1. Carla appears nervous.

2. She is the first singer on the program.

3. Last year she was last on the program.

4. Another performer is last this year.

5. The stage looks beautiful.

6. Flowers are everywhere.

7. The flowers smell fresh.

8. Carla feels ready to start.

9. Her song sounds wonderful.

10. The audience seems pleased.

 Complete each sentence with a linking verb from the box. You may use any verb more than once.

am	appeared	are	became	is	seemed	was	were

11. Thomas _____ frightened.

12. He _____ alone in the cabin for the first time.

13. In the dark forest, everything _____ threatening.

14. Because of the storm, the lights _____ out.

15. Even the shadows _____ strange.

16. "This _____ stupid," he thought.

17. "I _____ brave; I'm not a coward."

18. "Where _____ Aaron?" he wondered.

19. There _____ bears in the woods.

20. What if he _____ lost?

Language: Usage and Practice 7, SV 1419027840

Name _____   Date _____

Principal Parts of Verbs

- A verb has four principal parts: **present, present participle, past,** and **past participle.**
- For regular verbs, form the present participle by adding <u>ing</u> to the present. Use a form of the helping verb <u>be</u> with the present participle.
- Form the past and past participle by adding <u>ed</u> to the present. Use a form of the helping verb <u>have</u> with the past participle.

  EXAMPLES:

Present	Present Participle	Past	Past Participle
laugh	(is) laughing	laughed	(have, has, had) laughed
bake	(is) baking	baked	(have, has, had) baked
live	(is) living	lived	(have, has, had) lived

- Irregular verbs form their past and past participle in other ways. A dictionary shows the principal parts of these verbs.

 Write the present participle, past, and past participle for each verb.

PRESENT	PRESENT PARTICIPLE	PAST	PAST PARTICIPLE
1. stop	_____	_____	_____
2. listen	_____	_____	_____
3. carry	_____	_____	_____
4. help	_____	_____	_____
5. start	_____	_____	_____
6. borrow	_____	_____	_____
7. call	_____	_____	_____
8. receive	_____	_____	_____
9. hope	_____	_____	_____
10. illustrate	_____	_____	_____
11. divide	_____	_____	_____
12. change	_____	_____	_____
13. score	_____	_____	_____
14. iron	_____	_____	_____
15. study	_____	_____	_____
16. collect	_____	_____	_____
17. laugh	_____	_____	_____

Language: Usage and Practice 7, SV 1419027840

Name _____ Date _____

Verb Phrases

- A **verb phrase** consists of a main verb and one or more **helping verbs**.
- A helping verb is also called an **auxiliary verb**. In a verb phrase, the helping verb or verbs precede the main verb.
  - EXAMPLE: Michael **has arrived.**
- The helping verbs are:
  - am, are, is, was, were, be, being, been
  - has, have, had
  - do, does, did
  - can, could, must, may, might, shall, should, will, would

 Write a sentence using each word below as the main verb in a verb phrase.

1. gone _____

2. written _____

3. come _____

4. thrown _____

5. draw _____

6. walking _____

7. invent _____

8. sing _____

9. seen _____

10. eaten _____

 Underline the verb phrase in each sentence.

11. Isabel has returned from a vacation in Florida.

12. She has planned to tell us all about it.

13. Isabel would have answered every question about her trip.

14. Our club officers have been looking for someone to speak.

15. The officers have asked Isabel to the meeting.

16. They have organized an interesting meeting.

17. Every detail of the meeting has been planned carefully.

18. I must speak to Isabel immediately.

19. The lights were dimmed for Isabel's slide show.

20. She said that alligators had been seen in some places.

21. Pets and farm animals were threatened by them.

22. We are planning a trip to Florida next year.

Name _____ Date _____

Verb Tenses

- The **tense** of a verb tells the time of the action or being. There are three simple tenses: present, past, and future.
- **Present tense** tells about what is happening now.
    EXAMPLES: Conrad **is** busy. Conrad **studies** hard.
- **Past tense** tells about something that happened before.
    EXAMPLE: Conrad **was** sick yesterday.
- **Future tense** tells about something that will happen. The auxiliary verbs <u>will</u> and <u>shall</u> are used in future tense.
    EXAMPLES:
        Conrad **will take** the test tomorrow.
        I **shall keep** my word.

 Complete each sentence by writing a verb in the tense shown in parentheses.

1. (future)   Hilary _____ tomorrow.

2. (future)   Joe _____ her up at the airport.

3. (past)   We _____ the house yesterday.

4. (past)   Carl _____ reservations for tomorrow night.

5. (present)   Hilary _____ my friend.

6. (future)   We _____ very excited about Hilary's visit.

7. (present)   I _____ on a sightseeing tour.

8. (past)   Marta _____ Toby last week.

Write <u>present</u>, <u>past</u>, or <u>future</u> for the tense of each underlined verb.

9. Classes <u>will end</u> next month.   _____

10. We <u>studied</u> hard yesterday.   _____

11. Final exams <u>will start</u> soon.   _____

12. I <u>review</u> every evening.   _____

13. This method <u>worked</u> at midterm.   _____

14. I <u>got</u> A's on my tests then.   _____

15. Marly <u>studies</u> with me.   _____

16. We <u>will study</u> every evening this week.   _____

17. I hardly <u>studied</u> last year.   _____

18. My grades <u>showed</u> it, too.   _____

Language: Usage and Practice 7, SV 1419027840

Present Perfect and Past Perfect Tenses

- The **perfect tenses** express action that happened before another time or event.
- The **present perfect tense** tells about something that happened at an indefinite time in the past.
- The present perfect tense consists of <u>has</u> or <u>have</u> + the past participle.
  - EXAMPLES: I **have eaten** already. He **has eaten,** too.
- The **past perfect tense** tells about something that happened before something else in the past.
- The past perfect tense consists of <u>had</u> + the past participle.
  - EXAMPLE: I already **had eaten** when they arrived.

✳ Write <u>present perfect</u> or <u>past perfect</u> for the tense of the underlined verbs.

_____ 1. Mei <u>had completed</u> high school in June.

_____ 2. She <u>had gone</u> to college in Memphis before coming here.

_____ 3. Mei <u>has decided</u> that she likes her new college.

_____ 4. She <u>had been worried</u> that she wouldn't fit in.

_____ 5. Mei <u>has lived</u> in her house for eight months.

_____ 6 We <u>have tried</u> to make Mei feel welcome.

_____ 7. She <u>has told</u> us a great deal about Memphis.

_____ 8. We <u>had known</u> Memphis was an important city.

_____ 9. However, Mei <u>has described</u> things we never knew!

_____ 10. We <u>have decided</u> that we would like to visit Tennessee someday.

✳ Complete each sentence with <u>have</u>, <u>has</u>, or <u>had</u> to form the verb tense indicated in parentheses.

11. (present perfect)   The pitcher _____ left the mound.

12. (present perfect)   The coach and the catcher _____ talked to him.

13. (past perfect)   The coach _____ warned him to be careful.

14. (present perfect)   Jason _____ taken his place on the mound.

15. (past present)   Jason _____ pitched ten games by the end of last season.

16. (present perfect)   Jason _____ pitched very well.

17. (past perfect)   The team _____ won every game last week.

Using *Is/Are* and *Was/Were*

> - Use <u>is</u> and <u>was</u> with a singular subject.
>   EXAMPLE: Here **is** Roberto.
> - Use <u>are</u> and <u>were</u> with a plural subject.
>   EXAMPLE: There **are** Dr. Thomas and Dr. Williams.
> - Always use <u>are</u> and <u>were</u> with the pronoun <u>you</u>.
>   EXAMPLES:
>   You **are** my favorite cousin.
>   You **were** late yesterday.

 Circle the verb that agrees with the subject of each sentence.

1. Here (is, are) the box of paper clips you ordered.

2. There (is, are) three girls named Lori in our apartment building.

3. There (is, are) a small chance of showers tomorrow.

4. Mayor Laroche (is, are) going to speak today.

5. Here (is, are) the tools you asked me to bring.

6. There (is, are) much to be done.

7. Two of these chairs (is, are) damaged.

8. (Is, Are) these cars really being offered for sale?

9. Kelly, (is, are) this your car?

10. Many people (is, are) planning to go to the hockey game.

11. Juan and I (was, were) afraid that Carlos (was, were) not going to arrive on time.

12. Who (was, were) you talking to this afternoon?

13. A group of truck drivers (was, were) in the diner.

14. There (was, were) many kinds of rare plants in the garden.

15. Several visitors (was, were) here this afternoon.

16. Anita, (wasn't, weren't) you interested in working overtime?

17. Why (wasn't, weren't) these dishes washed last night?

18. The mistakes in punctuation (was, were) carefully checked.

19. Ahmad and Sara (wasn't, weren't) able to help us.

20. There (was, were) two large trays of sandwiches on the picnic table.

21. Each picture for the exhibit (was, were) carefully selected.

22. One of the sisters (was, were) enrolled at a university.

23. Each of the letters (was, were) read aloud.

24. (Was, Were) you planning to go to the park today?

25. Did you know that there (was, were) two new families in our apartment building?

26. (Wasn't, Weren't) you at the annual meeting, Ming?

27. Three of the people (was, were) injured when the accident occurred.

28. (Was, Were) your aunt and uncle the first to build a house on this block?

29. Who (was, were) the first settlers in your community?

Past Tenses of *Give, Take,* and *Write*

- Never use a helping verb with <u>gave</u>, <u>took</u>, and <u>wrote</u>.
- Always use a helping verb with <u>given</u>, <u>taken</u>, and <u>written</u>.

 Underline the correct verb in parentheses to complete each sentence.

1. It (took, taken) the mechanic only a few minutes to change the tire.

2. Has anyone (took, taken) my note pad?

3. Who (wrote, written) the best letter?

4. I have (wrote, written) a thank-you note.

5. Tell me who (gave, given) you that address.

6. Have you (gave, given) the dog its food?

7. Bill hadn't (wrote, written) this poem.

8. Have you finally (wrote, written) for the tickets?

9. Emilio had (gave, given) the lecture on boat safety yesterday at the Y.M.C.A.

10. Alicia and I (wrote, written) a letter to the editor.

11. Haven't you (took, taken) your seat yet?

12. We had our picture (took, taken) yesterday.

13. Who (gave, given) you these old magazines?

14. The workers (took, taken) all their equipment with them.

15. A friend had (gave, given) us the furniture.

16. Leslie had (wrote, written) the letter over three weeks ago.

17. Who (took, taken) the most photographs on the trip?

18. The doctor (gave, given) me a tetanus shot after I cut my hand.

19. Has Brian (wrote, written) to Julia yet?

Write the correct past tense form of each verb in parentheses to complete the sentences.

20. (take) Amanda recently _____ her dog, Ralph, to the veterinarian.

21. (write) The doctor had _____ to say that Ralph needed his annual shots.

22. (give) An assistant _____ Ralph a dog biscuit as soon as he arrived.

23. (give) That way Ralph was _____ something that would distract him.

24. (take) Before Ralph knew it, the doctor had _____ a sample of his blood.

25. (take) It only _____ a minute to give Ralph his shots.

26. (give) The doctor _____ Ralph a pat on the head.

27. (take) "You have _____ very good care of Ralph," he said.

Name _____ Date _____

Past Tenses of *See*, *Go*, and *Begin*

> • Never use a helping verb with <u>saw</u>, <u>went</u>, and <u>began</u>.
> • Always use a helping verb with <u>seen</u>, <u>gone</u>, and <u>begun</u>.

 Underline the correct verb in parentheses to complete each sentence.

1. The last person we (saw, seen) in the park was Erica.

2. Who has (went, gone) for the ice?

3. Kiara and Yoko (began, begun) to fix the flat tire.

4. Chuck (went, gone) to the supermarket for some lettuce.

5. Our summer vacation has (began, begun).

6. They had (saw, seen) a shooting star.

7. Hasn't she (went, gone) to the airport?

8. Yes, we (saw, seen) the concert poster.

9. Ava, have you ever (saw, seen) a penguin?

10. We never (went, gone) to hear the new mayor speak.

11. Olivia, why haven't you (began, begun) your work?

12. Mike (began, begun) to tell us about the accident.

13. Our guests have (went, gone).

14. It (began, begun) to snow early in the evening.

15. Work has finally (began, begun) on the new stadium.

16. We (saw, seen) Pikes Peak last summer.

17. My three sisters (went, gone) to Toronto, Ontario.

18. Have you (saw, seen) the waves pounding the huge boulders?

19. We (went, gone) to hear the symphony last night.

20. They (began, begun) their program with music by Mozart.

21. The program (began, begun) on time.

 Write a sentence using each verb below.

22. saw _____

23. seen _____

24. gone _____

25. went _____

26. began _____

27. begun _____

Language: Usage and Practice 7, SV 1419027840

Name _____ Date _____

Wear, Rise, Steal, Choose, and Break

> • Never use a helping verb with <u>wore</u>, <u>rose</u>, <u>stole</u>, <u>chose</u>, and <u>broke</u>.
> • Always use a helping verb with <u>worn</u>, <u>risen</u>, <u>stolen</u>, <u>chosen</u>, and <u>broken</u>.

 Underline the correct verb in parentheses to complete each sentence.

1. We almost froze because we hadn't (wore, worn) coats.

2. Haven't you (chose, chosen) a new shirt?

3. I (broke, broken) my new bike.

4. The river (rose, risen) two feet during the night.

5. Someone had (stole, stolen) our car last week.

6. Juanita had (chose, chosen) many of our old landmarks for the city tour.

7. I have (wore, worn) these uncomfortable shoes for the last time.

8. We were miles along the way when the sun (rose, risen).

9. The squirrels have (stole, stolen) most of our pecans.

10. The airplane (rose, risen) above the clouds.

11. The children have (wore, worn) a path through the backyard.

12. They (chose, chosen) to stay at the camp for a day.

13. Janna had (broke, broken) her leg the summer we visited her.

14. Have you ever (stole, stolen) home base?

15. Our pizza dough had (rose, risen) by the time we sliced the pepperoni.

16. The bottle's protective seal was (broke, broken), so we returned it to the store.

17. Kurt and Jamie (wore, worn) each other's clothes when they were younger.

18. The full moon had (rose, risen) over the deep, dark lake.

19. The jewel thief (stole, stolen) one too many diamonds before he got caught.

 Circle any mistakes in the use of past tense verbs.

     The sun had just rose when Kate recognized the familiar sound of fishing boats returning to shore. She hadn't meant to sleep late this morning, but the early morning waves had coaxed her back to sleep. Now, slipping into her sweatshirt, shorts, and damp shoes, Kate noticed that seagulls had again stole fish from the pail of bait. She chuckled at the thought and then tossed the circling birds another minnow. Turning, Kate noticed Luke nearing the boat. He worn the same windbreaker and soft, leather shoes nearly every day since they first met, months ago. Kate paused for a moment. It occurred to her that she chosen a good friend. Luke had never broke a shoestring, or a promise.

Unit 3: Grammar and Usage
Language: Usage and Practice 7, SV 1419027840

Come, Ring, Drink, Know, and Throw

- Never use a helping verb with <u>came</u>, <u>rang</u>, <u>drank</u>, <u>knew</u>, and <u>threw</u>.
- Always use a helping verb with <u>come</u>, <u>rung</u>, <u>drunk</u>, <u>known</u>, and <u>thrown</u>.

 Underline the correct verb in parentheses to complete each sentence.

1. The tired horse (drank, drunk) from the cool stream.

2. The church bell has not (rang, rung) today.

3. I haven't (drank, drunk) my hot chocolate.

4. We (knew, known) that it was time to go.

5. Have you (threw, thrown) the garbage out?

6. Haven't the movers (came, come) for our furniture?

7. We (rang, rung) the fire alarm five minutes ago.

8. Haven't you (know, known) him for a long time?

9. I (threw, thrown) the ball to Derrek.

10. My friends from London, England, (came, come) this afternoon.

11. Why haven't you (drank, drunk) your juice?

12. I always (came, come) to work in my wheelchair now.

13. I (knew, known) Pat when she was just a child.

14. Have you (threw, thrown) away last week's newspaper?

15. We have (came, come) to tell you something.

16. If you already (rang, rung) the bell, then you might try knocking.

17. Terrence thinks he (drank, drunk) something that made him ill.

 Write a sentence using each verb below.

18. came _____

19. come _____

20. rang _____

21. rung _____

22. threw _____

23. thrown _____

24. drank _____

25. drunk _____

26. knew _____

Language: Usage and Practice 7, SV 1419027840

Name _____   Date _____

Eat, Fall, Draw, Drive, and Run

> • Never use a helping verb with <u>ate</u>, <u>fell</u>, <u>drew</u>, <u>drove</u>, and <u>ran</u>.
> • Always use a helping verb with <u>eaten</u>, <u>fallen</u>, <u>drawn</u>, <u>driven</u>, and <u>run</u>.

 Underline the correct verb in parentheses to complete each sentence.

1. Taro, have you (drew, drawn) your diagram?

2. When we had (drove, driven) for two hours, we (began, begun) to feel hungry.

3. All of our pears have (fell, fallen) from the tree.

4. After we had (ate, eaten) our dinner, we (ran, run) around the lake.

5. A great architect (drew, drawn) the plans for our civic center.

6. We had just (ran, run) into the house when we saw our friends.

7. Hadn't the building already (fell, fallen) when you (ran, run) around the corner?

8. Those heavy curtains in the theater have (fell, fallen) down.

9. Last week we (drove, driven) to the lake for a vacation.

10. I have just (ate, eaten) a delicious slice of pizza.

11. I (ate, eaten) my breakfast before six o'clock this morning.

12. All of the leaves have (fell, fallen) from the elm trees.

13. When was the last time you (ran, run) a mile?

Write the correct past tense form of each verb in parentheses to complete the sentences.

14. (drive)   Last weekend we _____ to the lake for a picnic.

15. (draw)   Since Jenna knew several shortcuts, she _____ a detailed map for us.

16. (fall)   She mentioned that during a recent summer storm, debris had _____ on many of the roads.

17. (fall)   She warned us that a large tree _____ on one of the main roads.

18. (drive)   Jenna claimed that she had never _____ under such dangerous circumstances.

19. (run)   "I almost _____ right into that tree in the dark!" Jenna said.

20. (eat)   In order to avoid traveling at night, we _____ our dinner after we got home from the lake.

21. (eat)   We had _____ so much during our picnic that none of us minded waiting!

22. (draw)   Once home, we all agreed that Jenna had _____ a great map for us.

23. (run)   We made the trip in record time, and we hadn't _____ over any trees in the process!

Language: Usage and Practice 7, SV 1419027840

Forms of *Do*

- Never use a helping verb with <u>did</u>.
    - EXAMPLE: Anne **did** a great job on her test.
- Always use a helping verb with <u>done</u>.
    - EXAMPLE: Hallie **had** also **done** a great job.
- <u>Doesn't</u> is the contraction of <u>does not</u>. Use it with singular nouns and the pronouns <u>he</u>, <u>she</u>, and <u>it</u>.
    - EXAMPLES:
        - Rachel **doesn't** want to go.
        - It **doesn't** seem right.
- <u>Don't</u> is the contraction of <u>do not</u>. Use it with plural nouns and with the pronouns <u>I</u>, <u>you</u>, <u>we</u>, and <u>they</u>.
    - EXAMPLES:
        - Mr. and Mrs. Ricci **don't** live there.
        - You **don't** have your lunch.

 Underline the correct verb in parentheses to complete each sentence.

1. Why (doesn't, don't) Lois have the car keys?

2. Show me the way you (did, done) it.

3. Have the three of you (did, done) most of the work?

4. Why (doesn't, don't) she cash a check today?

5. Please show me what damage the storm (did, done).

6. (Doesn't, Don't) the workers on the morning shift do a fine job?

7. Have the new owners of our building (did, done) anything about the plumbing?

8. (Doesn't, Don't) those apples look overly ripe?

9. Chris (doesn't, don't) want to do the spring cleaning this week.

10. The gloves and the hat (doesn't, don't) match.

11. Carolyn, have you (did, done) your homework today?

12. Who (did, done) this fine job of painting?

13. (Doesn't, Don't) the tile in our new kitchen look nice?

14. (Doesn't, Don't) that dog stay in a fenced yard?

15. He has (did, done) me a great favor.

16. I will help if he (doesn't, don't).

 Write one sentence using <u>did</u> and one sentence using <u>done</u>.

17. _____

18. _____

 Write one sentence using <u>doesn't</u> and one sentence using <u>don't</u>.

19. _____

20. _____

Transitive and Intransitive Verbs

- There are two kinds of action verbs: **transitive** and **intransitive**.
- A transitive verb has a direct object.

    DO

    EXAMPLE: Jeffrey **painted** the house.
- An intransitive verb does not need an object to complete its meaning.

    EXAMPLES:

    The sun **rises** in the east.

    She **walks** quickly.

 Underline the verb in each sentence. Then write <u>T</u> for transitive or <u>I</u> for intransitive.

_____ 1. Kristina joined the health club in March.

_____ 2. She wanted the exercise to help her stay healthy.

_____ 3. Kristina exercised every day after work.

_____ 4. She became friendly with Neena.

_____ 5. They worked out together.

_____ 6. Neena preferred the treadmill.

_____ 7. Kristina liked aerobics and running.

_____ 8. Sometimes they switched activities.

_____ 9. Neena took an aerobics class.

_____ 10. Kristina used the treadmill.

_____ 11. Occasionally they swam in the pool.

_____ 12. Neena was the better swimmer.

_____ 13. But Kristina had more fun.

_____ 14. She just splashed around in the water.

Underline the transitive verb and circle the direct object in each sentence.

15. Carlos walked Tiny every day.

16. Tiny usually pulled Carlos along.

17. Carlos washed Tiny every other week.

18. Tiny loved water.

19. He splashed Carlos whenever he could.

20. Tiny also loved rawhide bones.

21. He chewed the bones until they were gone.

22. Carlos found Tiny when Tiny was just a puppy.

Verbals

- A **verbal** is a verb form that functions as a noun or adjective.
- There are three types of verbals: **infinitives, participles,** and **gerunds.**
- An **infinitive** is the base form of the verb, commonly preceded by <u>to</u>. An infinitive that functions as a noun is a verbal.
    - EXAMPLE: The object of the game is **to win.**
- A present or past **participle** that functions as an adjective is a verbal.
    - EXAMPLES:
        - A **running** horse galloped down the road.
        - **Dried** leaves flew from his hooves.
- A **gerund** is the present participle of a verb form ending in <u>ing</u> that is used as a noun.
    - EXAMPLE: **Skating** is her favorite sport.

 Underline the infinitive in each sentence below.

1. Alan refused to quit.

2. The only thing he wanted was to finish.

3. Alan had trained to run this race for months.

4. It was not important to win.

5. Alan simply needed to finish.

6. He hoped to accomplish his goal.

7. Soon he was close enough to see the finish line.

 Underline the participle in each sentence below.

8. A yelling cheerleader led the crowd.

9. The excited crowd roared.

10. The running team took the field.

11. The marching band started to play.

12. Chosen members of the band flashed cards.

13. The flashing cards spelled a message.

14. The interested students studied hard.

 Underline the gerund in each sentence below.

15. Studying is an important job.

16. Language arts and reading help improve your language ability.

17. Learning can be rewarding.

18. Memorizing is another skill you can learn.

19. Remembering is not always easy.

20. Do you think studying is time well spent?

21. Dancing is Lauren's favorite activity.

Verbals, p. 2

✳ **Underline the verbal in each sentence and write <u>infinitive</u>, <u>participle</u>, or <u>gerund</u> on the line.**

_____ **22.** To act in a play is an honor.

_____ **23.** Acting can be very exciting.

_____ **24.** To write plays takes a lot of skill.

_____ **25.** Working in the theater is interesting.

_____ **26.** Shari wanted to participate.

_____ **27.** The hurried director got ready for the auditions.

_____ **28.** Shari prepared a moving scene.

_____ **29.** She was finally ready to read her scene.

_____ **30.** Auditioning can scare anyone.

_____ **31.** Shari's stirring performance won her a part.

_____ **32.** Rehearsing can take up much time.

_____ **33.** The actors must work long hours to memorize their parts.

_____ **34.** Shari's convincing performance was outstanding.

_____ **35.** All of the actors excelled in performing.

_____ **36.** The smiling director congratulated the cast.

_____ **37.** "To act is an art," said the director.

_____ **38.** He called them all budding artists.

_____ **39.** Performing is a pleasure for Yolanda.

_____ **40.** Bowing is even more fun.

_____ **41.** The audience could tell by Yolanda's face that she enjoyed playing the part.

_____ **42.** To continue her studies is her goal.

_____ **43.** Acting is very important to Yolanda and Shari.

_____ **44.** Interrupted lessons would distress them both.

_____ **45.** They are consumed with acting.

_____ **46.** They need constant practice to excel.

_____ **47.** Well-rehearsed actors perform better.

Language: Usage and Practice 7, SV 1419027840

Active and Passive Voice

- **Voice** refers to the relation of a subject to its verb.
- In the **active voice,** the subject acts.
    - EXAMPLE: I **painted** the house.
- In the **passive voice,** the subject receives the action.
    - EXAMPLE: The house **was painted** by me.
- Only transitive verbs are used in the passive voice.

Write A if the sentence is in the active voice and P if it is in the passive voice.

_____ **1.** Marty applied for a job in a grocery store.

_____ **2.** He needs money for gas and car repairs.

_____ **3.** He will handle the cash register.

_____ **4.** Marty will also stock the shelves.

_____ **5.** The application was turned in last week.

_____ **6.** The store's manager reads every application.

_____ **7.** Then the applicants are interviewed.

_____ **8.** Marty was interviewed on Monday.

_____ **9.** The manager was impressed by Marty.

_____ **10.** He will give Marty the job.

Rewrite each sentence in the active voice.

11. Kaitlin was given a job babysitting by the McNeils.

_____

12. The children will be watched by her every day.

_____

13. Kaitlin will be driven to their house by her friend.

_____

Rewrite each sentence in the passive voice.

14. Trina plays the drums in the band.

_____

15. She chose the drums because her father played drums.

_____

16. Trina won an award for her playing.

_____

Name _____ Date _____

Pronouns

- A **subject pronoun** is used in the subject of a sentence and after a linking verb.
    EXAMPLES:
    We are going to the tournament.
    The woman in the suit is **she.**
- An **object pronoun** is used after an action verb or a preposition.
    EXAMPLE: Jerome threw the ball to **me.**
- A **possessive pronoun** is used to show ownership of something.
    EXAMPLES: The red shoes are **mine.** Those are **my** red shoes.
- An **indefinite pronoun** does not refer to a specific person or thing.
    EXAMPLE: **Someone** should take that history class.
- Use <u>who</u> as a subject pronoun, and use <u>whom</u> as an object pronoun.
    EXAMPLES:
    Who is going to the party?
    We will ask **whom** to go with us?

 Underline each correct pronoun.

1. LaTonya spoke to Jennifer and (I, me) about it.

2. Dean sent Todd and (they, them) some new shirts.

3. Please bring Anna and (I, me) some cool water.

4. Here comes (my, me) brother David.

5. Shia and (he, him) were late today.

6. Was it (she, her) who answered the knock?

7. I don't believe it was (they, them)!

8. Mona took Darrel and (we, us) to work.

9. He told Steven and (she, her) about the problem.

10. Don't you think (someone, us) should help?

11. Rosa and (I, me) are going to work until seven o'clock.

12. It wasn't (your, yours) cat that meowed.

13. (He, Him) and Cal are going to the game.

14. She told Mary Kate and (my, me) about her fishing trip.

15. (Who, Whom) did you say got here early?

16. He said that it was (they, them) who came to our house.

17. (Everyone, We) will carry his or her own bundles.

18. It was (they, their) babysitter who knocked on the door.

19. (Who, Whom) did you meet for lunch?

20. Elizabeth and (she, her) always sit together.

21. This sweater is (hers, she).

22. (Who, Whom) led the band in the parade?

23. The red car is (our, ours).

24. Can you predict (who, whom) will win the election?

Language: Usage and Practice 7, SV 1419027840

Pronouns, p. 2

 Underline each pronoun in these sentences.

25. I told you to speak to him about our fishing trip.

26. Who is speaking?

27. They saw us when we passed by their house.

28. Just between you and me, I want to go with them.

29. He and Ken are going with us.

30. My decision to leave was made before our conversation.

31. Whom did you see?

32. This package was sent to you and me.

33. They are going with us to the game.

34. Troy broke his arm.

35. Who told them?

36. She is my friend who moved to Mexico.

37. This check is mine.

38. Someone took some fresh flowers to them.

39. Who is she?

40. She went with us to the parade.

41. John, who is the president of that company?

42. Will she go with you?

43. Who telephoned me?

44. Should we eat with them at the picnic?

45. Which is your raincoat?

46. Did I tell you about our plans?

47. Which is mine?

48. Do you recall your sister's middle initial?

49. Why can't you come with us?

50. Did anybody get a letter?

51. You and I are on the list, too.

52. Did you see him?

 Write sentences using the following pronouns.

53. theirs _____

54. you and I _____

55. you and me _____

56. them _____

57. anyone _____

Unit 3: Grammar and Usage
Language: Usage and Practice 7, SV 1419027840

Antecedents

- An **antecedent** is the word to which a pronoun refers.
    EXAMPLE: **Dogs** are dangerous if **they** bite.
- A pronoun must agree with its antecedent in **gender** (masculine, feminine, or neuter) and in **number** (singular or plural).
    EXAMPLES:
      Ayla washed **her** hair.
      The **storm** changed **its** course.
      The **workers** went to **their** offices.
- If the antecedent is an indefinite pronoun (one that doesn't refer to a specific person or thing), it is correct to use a masculine pronoun. However, it is now common to use both a masculine and a feminine pronoun.
    EXAMPLES: Someone lost **his** gloves. Someone lost **his or her** gloves.

 Underline each pronoun. Circle its antecedent.

1. Micah said he would tutor Carmen.

2. Carmen was doing poorly in her math class.

3. Carmen often shakes her head in confusion.

4. Micah promised to try his hardest.

5. Carmen worked on her math, but it was difficult.

6. Micah and Carmen said they would work every night.

7. The math test was coming, and it promised to be hard.

8. The class was ready for its test.

9. Carmen's palms were sweaty, and they felt clammy.

10. The teacher said he knew Carmen would do well.

11. When Carmen started the test, it didn't seem so hard.

12. Each student finished his or her test and put it on the instructor's desk.

13. The instructor would correct the tests and hand them back.

14. Carmen was pleased with her grade.

 Circle the pronoun in parentheses that agrees with the antecedent.

15. Earl and Leon practiced (their, his) free throws.

16. Each hoped practice would make (him, them) play better.

17. The team held (its, their) practice every day.

18. Leon practiced (his, their) passing.

19. It is important to study the plays because (they, he) must be remembered.

20. Carlton waxed (him, his) car.

21. The building was closed because (its, their) windows were damaged in the storm.

22. The flowers opened (its, their) petals in the sunshine.

23. Maggie found (his, her) book in the closet.

24. The guests piled (their, them) coats on the table.

Language: Usage and Practice 7, SV 1419027840

Adjectives

- An **adjective** is a word that modifies a noun or a pronoun.
  EXAMPLE: He likes **chocolate** cookies.
- Adjectives usually tell what kind, which one, or how many.
  EXAMPLES: **shiny** penny   **those** oranges   **ten** classmates
- A **proper adjective** is an adjective that is formed from a proper noun. It always begins with a capital letter.
  EXAMPLES: **Asian** continent   **English** language
- The articles <u>a</u>, <u>an</u>, and <u>the</u> are called **limiting adjectives.**

 Write three adjectives to describe each noun.

1. mountains _____ _____ _____

2. weather _____ _____ _____

3. journey _____ _____ _____

4. classroom _____ _____ _____

5. book _____ _____ _____

Underline each adjective.

6. This old chair is comfortable.

7. We have read a funny story recently.

8. This heavy traffic creates many dangerous situations.

9. The eager sailors collected odd souvenirs at every port.

10. The tired, thirsty soldiers marched on.

11. This is my favorite book.

12. The solitary guard walked along the lonely beach.

13. We sat in the sixth row.

14. These damp matches will not strike.

15. Dan made French toast for breakfast.

16. Will you light those candles, please?

17. A red bird chirped loudly in the tall tree.

18. The heavy elephant sat down slowly.

19. A tour bus stopped at the pirate's cove.

20. The gorgeous model wore Italian leather.

21. We ate fresh seafood on our vacation.

22. Do you like mashed or baked potatoes?

23. She served Chinese food for dinner.

Name _____ Date _____

Demonstrative Adjectives

- A **demonstrative adjective** is one that points out a specific person or thing.
- <u>This</u> and <u>that</u> modify singular nouns. <u>This</u> points to a person or thing nearby, and <u>that</u> points to a person or thing farther away.
  EXAMPLES:
  This movie is my favorite.
  That sign is difficult to see.
- <u>These</u> and <u>those</u> modify plural nouns. <u>These</u> points to persons or things nearby, and <u>those</u> points to persons or things farther away.
  EXAMPLES:
  These ribbons are the most colorful.
  Those towels need to be folded.
- The word <u>them</u> is a pronoun. Never use it to describe a noun.

 Underline the correct demonstrative adjective in parentheses to complete each sentence.

1. Move (those, them) plants inside since it may freeze tonight.
2. (These, That) box in front of me is too heavy to lift.
3. Who brought us (those, them) delicious cookies?
4. Look at (those, them) playful kittens.
5. (That, Those) kind of friend is appreciated.
6. (Those, Them) pictures are beautiful.
7. What are (those, them) sounds I hear?
8. Did you ever meet (those, them) people?
9. We have just developed (these, them) photographs.
10. Do you know any of (those, them) young people?
11. May we take some of (these, them) folders?
12. I have been looking over (these, them) magazines.
13. Do not eat too many of (those, them) peaches.
14. I do not like (this, these) kind of syrup.
15. (Those, Them) people should be served next.
16. Jim Bob, please mail (these, them) letters.
17. Look at (those, them) posters I made!
18. (This, That) suburb is fifty miles away.
19. (These, Them) antique coins are valuable.
20. Look at (those, that) soccer players hustle!
21. Antonio, may we see (these, them) photographs?
22. Please return (that, these) library books.
23. (These, Them) clothes need to be washed.
24. Please hand me (that, those) plates.
25. (Those, Them) cookies have nuts in them.

Unit 3: Grammar and Usage
Language: Usage and Practice 7, SV 1419027840

Comparing with Adjectives

- An adjective has three degrees of comparison: **positive, comparative,** and **superlative.**
- The simple form of the adjective is called the **positive degree.**
    - EXAMPLE: Ian is **short.**
- When two people or things are being compared, the **comparative degree** is used.
    - EXAMPLE: Ian is **shorter** than Lee.
- When three or more people or things are being compared, the **superlative degree** is used.
    - EXAMPLE: Ian is the **shortest** person in the group.
- For all adjectives of one syllable and a few adjectives of two syllables, add <u>er</u> to form the comparative degree and <u>est</u> to form the superlative degree.
    - EXAMPLE: smart—smarter—smartest
- For some adjectives of two syllables and all adjectives of three or more syllables, use <u>more</u> or <u>less</u> to form the comparative and <u>most</u> or <u>least</u> to form the superlative.
    - EXAMPLES:
        - This test is **more difficult** than I expected.
        - Carlo is the **most generous** of all.
        - Kate is **less talkative** than Tom.
        - Mario is the **least talkative** of all.

 Complete each sentence with the correct degree of comparison of the adjective given in parentheses. Some of the forms are irregular.

1. (changeable)   The weather seems _____ this year than last.

2. (faithful)   I think the dog is the _____ of all animals.

3. (agreeable)   Is Janis _____ than Janet?

4. (busy)   Theresa is the _____ person in the office.

5. (long)   Which is the _____ river, the Mississippi or the Amazon?

6. (lovely)   I think the rose is the _____ of all flowers.

7. (fresh)   Show me the _____ cookies in the store.

8. (high)   Which of the two mountains is _____?

9. (enjoyable)   Which is the _____, television or the movies?

10. (reckless)   That person is the _____ driver in town.

11. (young)   Of all the players, Maria is the _____.

12. (tall)   Alberto is the _____ of the three men.

13. (difficult)   Isn't the seventh problem _____ than the eighth?

14. (quiet)   We have found the _____ spot in the park.

Name _____ Date _____

Adverbs

- An **adverb** is a word that modifies a verb, an adjective, or another adverb.
- An adverb usually tells how, when, where, or how often.
- Many adverbs end in <u>ly</u>.
    EXAMPLES:
        The rain poured **steadily.**
        His memories were **extremely** vivid.
        She responded very **quickly.**

 Underline each adverb.

1. The person read slowly but clearly and expressively.

2. Adam, you are driving too recklessly.

3. The airplane started moving slowly but quickly gained speed.

4. I spoke too harshly to my friends.

5. How did all of you get here?

6. I looked everywhere for my pen.

7. The man stopped suddenly and quickly turned around.

8. Stacy read that poem too rapidly.

9. Janice plays the guitar well.

10. The child was sleeping soundly.

11. The car was running noisily.

12. We returned early.

13. Those trees were severely damaged in the fire.

14. Jacob ran quickly, but steadily, in the race.

 Write two adverbs that could be used to modify each verb.

15. read _____ _____

16. think _____ _____

17. walk _____ _____

18. eat _____ _____

19. sing _____ _____

20. speak _____ _____

21. dive _____ _____

22. study _____ _____

23. write _____ _____

24. look _____ _____

Comparing with Adverbs

- An adverb has three degrees of comparison: **positive, comparative,** and **superlative.**
- The simple form of the adverb is called the **positive degree.**
    - EXAMPLE: Carl ran **fast** in the race.
- When two actions are being compared, the **comparative degree** is used.
    - EXAMPLE: Elvin ran **faster** than Carl.
- When three or more actions are being compared, the **superlative degree** is used.
    - EXAMPLE: Eleanor ran the **fastest** of all.
- Use <u>er</u> to form the comparative degree and <u>est</u> to form the superlative degree of one-syllable adverbs.
- Use <u>more</u> or <u>most</u> with longer adverbs and with adverbs that end in <u>ly</u>.
    - EXAMPLES:
        Lester ran **more energetically** than Bobbi Sue.
        Buster Baker ran the **most energetically** of all the runners.

 Underline the adverb that best completes each sentence.

1. Marco arrived (sooner, soonest) than Gregorio.

2. Tony Taylor arrived the (sooner, soonest) of all.

3. They had to work very (hard, harder, hardest).

4. Karina painted (more, most) carefully than Marco.

5. Marco worked (faster, fastest) than Lester, so Marco painted the walls.

6. Lauren worked the (more, most) carefully of all.

 Complete each sentence with the proper form of the adverb in parentheses.

7. (fast)   Jason wanted to be the _____ runner at our school.

8. (fast)   Juan could run _____ than Jason.

9. (seriously)   Jason trained _____ than he had before.

10. (frequently)   Jason is on the track _____ of all the runners.

11. (quickly)   Jason ran the sprint _____ than he did yesterday.

12. (promptly)   Jason arrives for practice _____ of anyone on the team.

13. (promptly)   He even arrives _____ than the coach!

14. (eagerly)   Juan does warm-up exercises _____ of all the runners.

15. (carefully)   Who concentrates _____ on his timing, Juan or Jason?

16. (hard)   The coach congratulates Jason on being the player who works the

_____.

Prepositions

- A **preposition** is a word that shows the relationship of a noun or a pronoun to another word in the sentence.
  EXAMPLES:
  The child ran **into** the **house.**
  He put his boots **under** the **table.**
- These are some commonly used prepositions:

about	against	at	between	from	of	through	under
above	among	behind	by	in	on	to	upon
across	around	beside	for	into	over	toward	with

 Underline each preposition in the sentences below.

1. Can you draw a map of your area?

2. Who is the owner of this car?

3. The pecan is a common tree in the South.

4. For whom are you waiting?

5. At the meeting, he spoke to me about your athletic ability.

6. Our company is proud of its industrious employees.

7. Her friend Cynthia stood beside her.

8. A small amount of that soup is all I want.

9. We went to the house at the end of the street.

10. There were seventy-five post offices in the United States in 1790.

11. Most of the spectators stood during the last quarter of the game.

12. These shoes of mine are too tight at the heel.

13. We ate dinner at the new restaurant near the river.

14. They stood on the porch and watched for the mail carrier.

15. Anyone can succeed with hard work.

16. We walked behind that group.

17. Astronaut Sally Ride was the first American woman in space.

18. A group of people on horses rode behind the band.

19. We walked to the picnic grounds during the lunch hour.

20. Ben slid down the slippery hill.

21. There is a bridge across the river in our town.

22. The ball was knocked over the fence and into the pond.

23. I see a spot of dirt under your left eye.

24. One can observe a strange world below the surface of an ocean.

25. The rocket quickly disappeared behind the clouds.

26. Much of our land is drained by the Mississippi River.

27. Please sit between us.

28. This package is for you.

Language: Usage and Practice 7, SV 1419027840

Prepositional Phrases

- A **phrase** is a group of closely related words used as a single part of speech but not containing a subject and predicate.
    - EXAMPLE: The writer **of this novel** is signing autographs.
- A **prepositional phrase** is a group of words that begins with a preposition and ends with a noun or pronoun.
    - EXAMPLE: He took the train **to New York.**
- The noun or pronoun in the prepositional phrase is called the **object of the preposition.**
    - EXAMPLE: He took the train to **New York.**

 Put parentheses around each prepositional phrase. Then underline each preposition and circle the object of the preposition.

1. The airplane was flying (above the clouds).
2. We are moving to North Carolina.
3. Secor lives on the second block.
4. An old water tower once stood on that hill.
5. The car slid on the wet pavement.
6. Sealing wax was invented in the seventeenth century.
7. Motto rings were first used by the Romans.
8. Tungsten, a metal, was discovered in 1781.
9. Roses originally came from Asia.
10. The ball rolled into the street.
11. Do you always keep the puppies in a pen?
12. The children climbed over the fence.
13. She lives in Denver, Colorado.
14. Columbus made three trips to North America.
15. They spread the lunch under the shade of the giant elm tree.
16. The treasure was found by a scuba diver.
17. A squad of soldiers marched behind the tank.
18. Shall I row across the stream?
19. Large airplanes fly across the nation.
20. Walter looked into the sack.
21. The cat ran up the pole.
22. We visited the Alexander Graham Bell Museum in Nova Scotia.
23. Many tourists come to our region.
24. We spent last summer in the Adirondack Mountains.
25. Do not stand behind a parked car.

Prepositional Phrases as Adjectives and Adverbs

- A prepositional phrase can be used to describe a noun or a pronoun.
- Then the prepositional phrase is being used as an adjective to tell which one, what kind, or how many.
  EXAMPLE: The bird **in the tree** whistled.
  The prepositional phrase in the tree tells **which** bird.
- A prepositional phrase can be used to describe a verb.
- Then the prepositional phrase is being used as an adverb to tell how, where, or when.
  EXAMPLE: Carri ate breakfast **before leaving her house**.
  The prepositional phrase before leaving her house tells **when** Carri ate breakfast.

Underline each prepositional phrase and classify it by writing adjective or adverb.

_____ 1. They went to the ranch.

_____ 2. The first savings bank was established in France.

_____ 3. Fall Creek Falls in Tennessee is my home.

_____ 4. Return all books to the public library.

_____ 5. Mark lives in an old house.

_____ 6. Tanya bought a sweater with red trim.

_____ 7. The birds in the zoo are magnificent.

_____ 8. Jade is found in Asia.

_____ 9. I spent the remainder of my money.

_____ 10. The magician waved a wand over the hat, and a rabbit appeared.

_____ 11. The diameter of a Sequoia tree trunk can reach ten feet.

_____ 12. The capital of New York is Albany.

_____ 13. The narrowest streets are near the docks.

_____ 14. Our family went to the movie.

_____ 15. Roald Amundsen discovered the South Pole in 1911.

_____ 16. The floor in this room is painted black.

_____ 17. The dead leaves are blowing across the yard.

_____ 18. A forest of petrified wood has been found.

_____ 19. The mole's tunnel runs across the lawn.

Conjunctions

> - A **conjunction** is a word used to join words or groups of words.
>   EXAMPLES:
>   Yuri **and** Brant have arrived.
>   They worked **until** the sun went down.
> - These are some commonly used conjunctions:
>
> | | | | | | | |
> |---|---|---|---|---|---|---|
> | although | because | however | or | that | until | whether |
> | and | but | if | since | though | when | while |
> | as | for | nor | than | unless | whereas | yet |
>
> - Some conjunctions are used in pairs. These include either . . . or,
>   neither . . . nor, and not only . . . but also.

 Underline each conjunction in the sentences below.

1. Do you know whether Brandon is going to the employment office?

2. Jesse, are you and Ryan going to see a movie this afternoon?

3. Melinda will go to the coast when the weather turns warm.

4. Gina or Vicki will take me to practice.

5. Are you and Lizbeth going swimming this Saturday?

6. Paulie will be here unless he has to work.

7. Dean or I must go to the supermarket.

8. Chicken and potatoes are my favorite foods.

9. The trainer and the animals gave a good show.

10. I was angry at Megan because she was not on time.

11. Ted gets into trouble, but he usually gets out of it.

12. Carelessness is the cause of many falls and burns.

13. She stopped work because she had to leave early.

14. Matt has been understanding since I started working two jobs.

15. This chair is small, but it is comfortable.

16. Although it looked like rain, we went for a drive.

17. Kerry is two years older than Cary.

18. The remark was neither just nor kind.

19. You may go either by bus or by plane.

20. Edward is here, but he is too busy to help us right now.

21. Let's go inside, for it is getting dark.

22. We listened closely while the directions were given.

23. Fruit is not only delicious but also healthful.

24. Bring either a short poem or a rhyme to class tomorrow.

25. Anya neither asked for help nor received any.

26. Neither Nicki nor Nathaniel went to the show.

Unit 3 Test

Darken the circle by the type of noun underlined in each sentence.

1. Alaska is a cold and icy state.   Ⓐ common   Ⓑ proper

2. Its land has sparse vegetation.   Ⓐ common   Ⓑ proper

3. Glaciers hold much fresh water.   Ⓐ common   Ⓑ proper

4. Juneau is the capital of Alaska.   Ⓐ common   Ⓑ proper

Darken the circle by the correct plural form of each underlined noun.

5. half
   Ⓐ halves
   Ⓑ halfs
   Ⓒ halfes

6. piano
   Ⓐ pianoes
   Ⓑ piano's
   Ⓒ pianos

7. brush
   Ⓐ brushes
   Ⓑ brushs
   Ⓒ brush's

Darken the circle by the sentences that contain an appositive or an appositive phrase.

8. Ⓐ Although we were tired, we were happy.
   Ⓑ After Carmen left, the rest of us played a game.
   Ⓒ Hearts, the game we chose, is a card game.
   Ⓓ As usual, Erica won.

9. Ⓐ Craig, an artist, drew my picture.
   Ⓑ He asked my friend to pose next.
   Ⓒ After he finished, he gave us the drawings.
   Ⓓ They were funny cartoons of us, and we laughed.

Darken the circle by the correct verb or verb phrase to complete each sentence.

10. This trail _____ to the park ranger's outpost.   Ⓐ leads   Ⓑ lead   Ⓒ is led

11. The first thing we _____ was clean up.   Ⓐ do   Ⓑ did   Ⓒ done

12. I know you _____ that movie already.   Ⓐ have seen   Ⓑ see   Ⓒ are seeing

13. Suddenly it _____ to rain heavily.   Ⓐ begun   Ⓑ began   Ⓒ begin

14. They _____ before the sun.   Ⓐ rising   Ⓑ risen   Ⓒ rose

15. Haven't you _____ your tea?   Ⓐ drank   Ⓑ drinking   Ⓒ drunk

16. I had _____ out of gas.   Ⓐ run   Ⓑ ran   Ⓒ running

17. He _____ his own car.   Ⓐ drove   Ⓑ drive   Ⓒ driven

Darken the circle by the sentence that contains an infinitive, a participle, or a gerund.

18. Ⓐ I swam this afternoon.
    Ⓑ Are you going to today's race?
    Ⓒ Dancing is a good form of exercise.

19. Ⓐ The leaves had fallen off the tree.
    Ⓑ I wasn't going to the party.
    Ⓒ I hope to win a scholarship for college.

Darken the circle by the sentence in which the pronoun agrees with its antecedent.

20. Ⓐ Both boys wrote his editorial for the paper.
    Ⓑ The topic was chosen because of their relevance.
    Ⓒ The paper printed both letters in its opinion section.

Unit 3 Test, p. 2

Darken the circle by the correct pronoun to complete each sentence.

21. Have you seen _____ new houses?   Ⓐ these   Ⓑ them   Ⓒ that   Ⓓ this

22. _____ and Patrick will debate today.   Ⓐ She   Ⓑ Them   Ⓒ Her   Ⓓ Us

23. You gave the prize to _____?   Ⓐ who   Ⓑ she   Ⓒ whom   Ⓓ they

24. Isabel already showed _____ her pictures.   Ⓐ them   Ⓑ they   Ⓒ I   Ⓓ she

25. Ginny rode with Martin and _____.   Ⓐ she   Ⓑ I   Ⓒ we   Ⓓ me

26. He told Alex's and _____ parents.   Ⓐ mine   Ⓑ my   Ⓒ us   Ⓓ hers

27. _____ needs to fix that.   Ⓐ We   Ⓑ They   Ⓒ Someone   Ⓓ I

28. The black dog is _____.   Ⓐ ours   Ⓑ our   Ⓒ she   Ⓓ their

Darken the circle by the correct form of the adjective or adverb to complete each sentence.

29. These are the _____ cookies I've ever tasted.   Ⓐ delicious   Ⓑ most delicious   Ⓒ more delicious

30. We left _____ than Ling did to avoid the traffic.   Ⓐ earlier   Ⓑ earliest   Ⓒ more early

31. She wanted to read a _____ book than her last one.   Ⓐ funny   Ⓑ funnier   Ⓒ funniest

32. The new heater runs _____ than our old one.   Ⓐ most efficiently   Ⓑ efficiently   Ⓒ more efficiently

33. Walnut and Elm are the _____ streets in the city.   Ⓐ busiest   Ⓑ busy   Ⓒ busier

34. French is _____ to learn than Spanish.   Ⓐ most difficult   Ⓑ difficult   Ⓒ more difficult

Darken the circle by the way the prepositional phrase is used in the sentence.

35. I spent my two-week vacation in Brazil.   Ⓐ as an adjective   Ⓑ as an adverb   Ⓒ not a prepositional phrase

36. We saw almost every kind of tropical animal.   Ⓐ as an adjective   Ⓑ as an adverb   Ⓒ not a prepositional phrase

37. I met a family from Spain.   Ⓐ as an adjective   Ⓑ as an adverb   Ⓒ not a prepositional phrase

38. They told me about the language differences.   Ⓐ as an adjective   Ⓑ as an adverb   Ⓒ not a prepositional phrase

39. Portuguese and Spanish only sound similar.   Ⓐ as an adjective   Ⓑ as an adverb   Ⓒ not a prepositional phrase

Darken the circle by the conjunction or conjunctions in each sentence.

40. Salad is not only good but also good for you.   Ⓐ only   Ⓑ for   Ⓒ not only . . . but also

41. Eating green and yellow vegetables can help you stay healthy.   Ⓐ can   Ⓑ and   Ⓒ you

42. Kamal was mad because I was so late.   Ⓐ because   Ⓑ so   Ⓒ late

     Language: Usage and Practice 7, SV 1419027840

Name _____ Date _____

Using Capital Letters

- Capitalize the first word of a sentence and of each line of poetry.
  EXAMPLES: Jim recited a poem. The first two lines follow.
             All the animals looked up in wonder
             When they heard the roaring thunder.
- Capitalize the first word of a direct quotation.
  EXAMPLE: Jennifer said, "Let's try to memorize a poem, too."
- Capitalize the first, last, and all important words in the titles of books, poems, stories, and songs.
  EXAMPLES: *The Jungle Book*, "Snow Time"

 Circle each letter that should be capitalized. Write the capital letter above it.

1. Zack said, "what time does the movie start?"

2. francis Scott Key wrote "the star-spangled banner."

3. edgar Allan Poe, the author of "the raven," was born in Boston.

4. paul asked, "when do you plan to visit your friend?"

5. who wrote the poems "snowbound" and "the barefoot boy"?

6. what famous American said, "give me liberty, or give me death"?

- Capitalize all proper nouns.
  EXAMPLES: James T. White, Mother, Fifth Avenue, Italy, Missouri,
             Smoky Mountains, Thanksgiving, November, Statue of Liberty,
             Mayflower, British Columbia
- Capitalize all proper adjectives. A proper adjective is an adjective that is made from a proper noun.
  EXAMPLES: the **Italian** language   **Chinese** food   **French** tourists

 Circle each letter that should be capitalized. Write the capital letter above it.

7. Lauren, does your friend live in miami, florida, or atlanta, georgia?

8. The potomac river forms the boundary between virginia and maryland.

9. The *pinta*, the *niña*, and the *santa maria* were the ships columbus sailed.

10. The spanish explorers discovered the mississippi river before the english settlers landed

    at jamestown.

11. The founder of the american red cross was clara barton.

12. Glaciers are found in the rocky mountains, the andes mountains, and the alps.

Name _____ Date _____

Using Capital Letters, p. 2

> - Capitalize a person's title when it comes before a name.
>   EXAMPLES: Mayor Flynn, Doctor Suarez, Governor Kuhn
> - Capitalize abbreviations of titles.
>   EXAMPLES: Ms. C. Cooke, Dr. Pearsoll, Gov. Milne, Sen. Kennedy

 Circle each letter that should be capitalized. Write the capital letter above it.

13. How long have you been seeing dr. thompson?

14. Our class invited mayor thomas to speak at graduation.

15. dr. crawford w. long of Georgia is believed to be the first physician to use ether during surgery.

16. What time do you expect mr. and mrs. randall to arrive?

17. Most people believe senator dixon will win reelection.

18. It will be a close election unless gov. alden gives his support.

19. When is ms. howell scheduled to begin teaching?

> - Capitalize abbreviations of days and months, parts of addresses, and titles of members of the armed forces.
> - Also capitalize all letters in the abbreviations of states.
>   EXAMPLES: Tues.; Oct.; 201 S. Second St.; Maj. Donna C. Plunkett; Boston, MA

 Circle each letter that should be capitalized. Write the capital letter above it.

20. niles school art fair

sat., feb. 8th, 9 A.M.

110 n. elm dr.

21. shoreville water festival

june 23–24

mirror lake

shoreville, mn 55108

22. october fest

october 28 and 29

9 A.M.–5 P.M.

63 maple st.

23. barbara dumont

150 telson rd.

markham, ontario L3R 1E5

24. captain c. j. neil

c/o *ocean star*

p.o. box 4455

portsmouth, nh 03801

25. dr. charles b. stevens

elmwood memorial hospital

1411 first street

tuscon, az 85062

Name _____ Date _____

Using Capital Letters, p. 3

 Write a sentence to show each use of capital letters.

26. Name of a holiday _____

_____

27. Name of a restaurant in your community _____

_____

28. Name of a favorite book _____

_____

29. Name of an author _____

_____

30. Name of a business firm in or near your community _____

_____

31. Name of a country _____

_____

32. Name of a song _____

_____

33. Name of a magazine _____

_____

34. A direct quotation _____

_____

35. Name of a musician _____

_____

36. A title that is written as part of a name _____

_____

37. Name of a college or university _____

_____

38. Name of a river or lake _____

_____

39. Name of an actor or actress _____

_____

Language: Usage and Practice 7, SV 1419027840

Name _____ Date _____

Using End Punctuation

> • Use a **period** at the end of a declarative sentence.
>   EXAMPLE: Sunlight is essential for the growth of plants.
> • Use a **question mark** at the end of an interrogative sentence.
>   EXAMPLE: How much sunlight does a plant need?

 Use a period or question mark to end each sentence below.

1. Doesn't Sandra's family now live in Missouri____

2. "Snow Time" is a well-known poem____

3. Isn't someone knocking at the door, Bette____

4. Didn't Janice ask us to meet her at 2:30 this afternoon____

5. In Yellowstone Park, we saw Morning Glory Pool, Handkerchief Pool, and Old Faithful____

6. The greatest library in ancient times was in Alexandria, Egypt____

7. Aren't the employees' checks deposited in a different bank____

8. Will Ms. Wilson start interviewing applicants at 10:00 A.M.____

9. My uncle has moved to Calgary, Alberta____

10. Corn, oats, and soybeans are grown in Iowa____

11. Isn't Alex the chairperson of our committee____

12. I've mowed the lawn, pulled the weeds, and raked the leaves____

13. Did the American Revolution begin on April 19, 1775____

14. Is El Salvador in Central America____

 Add the correct end punctuation where needed in the paragraphs below.

Did you know that experts say dogs have been around for thousands of years____ In fact,
they were the first animals to be made domestic____ The ancestors of dogs were hunters____
Wolves are related to domestic dogs____ Like wolves, dogs are social animals and prefer to
travel in groups____ This is called pack behavior____

There have been many famous dogs throughout history____ Can you name any of them____
In the eleventh century, one dog, Saur, was named king of Norway____ The actual king was
angry because his people had removed him from the throne, so he decided to make them
subjects of the dog____ The first dog in space was a Russian dog named Laika____ Laika
was aboard for the 1957 journey of *Sputnik*____ Most people have heard of Rin Tin Tin and
Lassie____ These dogs became famous in movies and television____

There are several hundred breeds of dogs throughout the world____ The smallest is the
Chihuahua____ A Chihuahua weighs less than two pounds____ Can you think of the largest____
A Saint Bernard or a mastiff can weigh over 150 pounds____

Name _____ Date _____

Using End Punctuation, p. 2

- Use a **period** at the end of an imperative sentence.
  - EXAMPLE: Open this jar of tomatoes for me, please.
- Use an **exclamation point** at the end of an exclamatory sentence and after an interjection that shows strong feelings.
- If a command expresses great excitement, use an exclamation point at the end of the sentence.
  - EXAMPLES: Look at the stars!   Ouch!   I'm so excited!

 Add periods or exclamation points where needed in the sentences below.

15. Answer the telephone, Michael____

16. Please clean the kitchen for me____

17. Oh____ I can't believe how late it is____

18. Hurry____ The plane is leaving in a few minutes____

19. Carry the bags to the check-in counter____

20. Then run to the waiting area____

21. Hold that seat for me____

22. I can't miss the flight____

23. Stop____ Stop____ You forgot your ticket____

24. Please slow down____

25. Sit down and put on your seat belt____

26. We're off____

27. Look how small the city is____

28. Please put on your seat belt____

29. Obey the captain's orders____

30. I can't wait until we land____

31. Please give me that magazine____

32. Look____ We're about to land____

 Add the correct end punctuation where needed in the paragraphs below.

Mr. Henry Modine lives in San Francisco, California____ He often exclaims, "What a wonderful town____" What do you think he does for a living____ Mr. Modine owns a fishing boat, *The Marlin*____ In all of San Francisco, there are few boats as fine as *The Marlin*____ Henry Modine named his boat after the fish his customers like the best—the marlin____ Henry guarantees his customers a fish if they come out on his boat____

"Fantastic____" shouts Henry when someone hooks a marlin____ Henry then says, "Bring it in____" Part of Henry's job is to help the fishers reel in the big fish____ Can you believe that some marlins weigh 1,000 pounds or more____ Most of the ones Henry's customers catch weigh about 100 pounds____ They are either striped marlins or black marlins____

Language: Usage and Practice 7, SV 1419027840

Name _____   Date _____

Using Commas

> • Use a **comma** between words or groups of words that are in a series.
>   EXAMPLE: Pears, peaches, plums, and figs grow in the southern states.
> • Use a comma before a conjunction in a compound sentence.
>   EXAMPLE: The farmers planted many crops, and they will work long hours
>   to harvest them.
> • Use a comma after a subordinate clause when it begins a sentence.
>   EXAMPLE: After we ate dinner, we went to a movie.

 Add commas where needed in the sentences below.

1. Frank Mary and Patricia are planning a surprise party for their parents.

2. It is their parents' fiftieth wedding anniversary and the children want it to be special.

3. They have invited the people their father used to work with their mother's garden club members and long-time friends of the family.

4. Even though the children are grown and living in their own homes it will be hard to make it a surprise.

5. Mr. and Mrs. Slaughter are active friendly and involved in many things.

6. For the surprise to work everyone will have to be sure not to say anything about their plans for that day.

7. This will be especially hard for the Knudsens but they will do their best.

8. Since every Sunday the families have dinner together the Knudsens will have to become very good actors the week of the party.

> • Use a comma to set off a quotation from the rest of a sentence.
>   EXAMPLES: "I want to go with you," said Paula.
>   Paula said, "I want to go with you."

 Add commas before or after the quotations below.

9. "We're sorry that we have to cancel our plans" said Earl.

10. Carmelita said "But we've done this every week for ten years!"

11. Jeanie said "We have to leave town."

12. Ivan asked "Can't you put it off just one day?"

13. "I'm afraid we can't" said Earl.

14. "Then we'll just start over the following week" said Carmelita cheerfully.

15. Jeanie said "I bet no one else has done this."

16. "I sure hate to spoil our record" said Earl.

17. "Don't worry about it" said Ivan.

18. "Everything will work out" said Jeanie.

Language: Usage and Practice 7, SV 1419027840

Using Commas, p. 2

> • Use a comma to set off the name of a person who is being addressed.
>   EXAMPLE: Amelia, are you ready to go?
> • Use a comma to set off words such as yes, no, well, and oh at the beginning of
>   a sentence.
>   EXAMPLE: Yes, we can go as soon as I find my jacket.
> • Use a comma to set off an appositive.
>   EXAMPLE: Felix, Amelia's dog, is entered in a dog show.

 Add commas where needed in the sentences below.

19. Anthony a grocery store owner was planning for a busy day.

20. "Diane would you open the store at 9 o'clock?" said Anthony.

21. "Of course that's the time we always open" said Diane.

22. "Pierre the chef at Elaine's will be coming by" he said.

23. Kelly said "Alicia I'd like some fresh peanuts."

24. "Yes but how many pounds would you like?" answered Alicia.

25. Ms. Harmon asked "Martin what kind of fresh fruit do you have?"

26. "Well let me check what came in this afternoon" said Martin.

27. Alvin the butcher had to wait on fifteen customers.

28. "I don't have time to wait Alvin" said Caroline.

29. The manager Juan told everyone to be patient.

30. "Please it will go quickly if you all take a number" said Juan.

31. "Yes you're right as usual" said the crowd.

32. Martin the produce manager went behind the counter to help.

33. Well they had sold all of their grapes and tomatoes before noon.

34. "We only have one bushel of green beans left" said Martin.

35. Mr. Loster bought cherries bananas and corn.

36. He was planning a special dinner for Sara his wife.

37. Mr. Loster spent the afternoon cooking baking and cleaning.

38. Today July 18 was her birthday.

 Add commas where needed in the paragraph below.

Men women boys and girls from across the nation participate in the Special Olympics.
Because of this event patterned after the Olympic games boys and girls with disabilities
have opportunities to compete in a variety of sports. The Special Olympics includes competition
in track swimming and gymnastics. Volunteers plan carefully and they work hard to ensure
that the event will be challenging rewarding and worthwhile for all the participants. One of
my neighbors Chris Bell once worked as a volunteer. "It was an experience that I'll never
forget" he said.

Name _____   Date _____

Using Quotation Marks and Apostrophes

- Use **quotation marks** to show the exact words of a speaker.
- Use a comma or another punctuation mark to separate the quotation from the rest of the sentence.
- A quotation may be placed at the beginning or at the end of a sentence. Begin the quotation with a capital letter.
    - EXAMPLES: Pat said, "Please take the dog for a walk."
      "Please take the dog for a walk," said Pat.
- A quotation may also be divided within the sentence.
    - EXAMPLE: "Pat," said Scott, "I just returned from a walk."

 Add quotation marks and commas where needed in the sentences below.

1. Wait for me said Lora because I want to go with you.

2. Kim, did you write an article about spacecraft? asked Kyle.

3. Where is the manager's desk? inquired the stranger.

4. Joanne asked What is Eric's address?

5. Davis asked How long did Queen Victoria rule the British Empire?

6. Carlos, did you bring your interesting article? asked the teacher.

7. Good morning said Cindi.

8. Jasmine asked Did Jules hurt himself when he fell?

9. The meeting begins in ten minutes said Rico.

10. Hoan, you're early said Melissa.

11. Come on, said the coach you'll have to play harder to win this game!

12. Shannon said, I know you'll do well in your new job. You're a hard worker.

- Use an **apostrophe** in a contraction to show where a letter or letters have been taken out.
    - EXAMPLES: I can't remember your name.   I'll have to think about it.
- Use an apostrophe to form a possessive noun. Add 's to most singular nouns. Add ' to most plural nouns. Add 's to a few nouns that have irregular plurals.
    - EXAMPLES: **Dina's** house is made of brick.
      All the **neighbors'** houses are wooden.
      The **children's** treehouse is wooden.

 Write the words in which an apostrophe has been left out. Insert apostrophes where they are needed.

13. Karen, didnt you want Shays job? _____

14. Havent you seen Darrens apartment? _____

15. Mitchell didnt hurt himself when he fell off Larrys ladder. _____

16. The employees paychecks didnt arrive on time. _____

Name _____   Date _____

Using Colons and Hyphens

> - Use a **colon** after the greeting in a business letter.
>   EXAMPLES: Dear Mr. Johnson: Dear Sirs:
> - Use a colon between the hour and the minute when writing the time.
>   EXAMPLES: 1:30   6:15   11:47
> - Use a colon to introduce a list.
>   EXAMPLE: Our grocery list included the following items: chicken, milk,
>   eggs, and broccoli.

 Add colons where needed in the sentences below.

1. At 2 1 0 this afternoon, the meeting will start.

2. Please bring the following materials with you pencils, paper, erasers, and a notebook.

3. The meeting should be over by 4 3 0.

4. Those of you on the special committee should bring the following items cups, paper plates, forks, spoons, and napkins.

5. The meeting will deal with the following pool hours, swimming rules, and practice schedules.

6. The lifeguards will meet this evening from 8 0 0 to 1 0 0 0 to discuss responsibilities.

7. We will read the letter at 3 0 0 and have a question-and-answer session.

> - Use a **hyphen** between the parts of some compound words.
>   EXAMPLES: twenty-one   sister-in-law   go-getter   well-behaved
>   air-conditioned   middle-aged   sixty-six   great-grandfather
>   blue-green   old-fashioned   second-story   ninety-two
> - Use a hyphen to separate the syllables of a word that is carried over from one line to the next.
>   EXAMPLE: When the coach has finished his speech, the class mem-
>   bers will be allowed to use the pool.

 Add hyphens where needed in the sentences below.

8. We decided to attend a class on how to use less water when garden

    ing in our backyard.

9. Our lawn and old fashioned flower gardens need too much water.

10. The sign up sheet at the door was for those who wanted to be on a mailing list.

11. Twenty seven people had already signed up.

12. We saw that our son and daughter in law were there, too.

13. Hank spotted them sitting on an aisle near the center of the audi

    torium.

14. The speaker was a well known expert on gardening.

15. We sat next to our family and learned about long term plans for water conservation.

Name _____ Date _____

Unit 4 Test

Darken the circle by the sentence in which a capital letter is needed.

1. Ⓐ Have you read *Nature's way*?
   Ⓑ Spanish is his native language.
   Ⓒ The judge ran for re-election.
   Ⓓ Their anniversary is in May.

2. Ⓐ Jesse lost the directions.
   Ⓑ His favorite sandwich is italian meatball.
   Ⓒ I called for a doctor's appointment.
   Ⓓ The television station went off the air.

3. Ⓐ Please leave me alone.
   Ⓑ The children remained calm.
   Ⓒ It got cold early this fall.
   Ⓓ where is the cheese I just bought?

4. Ⓐ February 25, 2007
   Ⓑ Dear friend,
   Ⓒ Toronto, ontario
   Ⓓ Yours truly,

5. Ⓐ "The Sounds of Silence"
   Ⓑ "Alan," said Teresa, "don't move."
   Ⓒ Frank said, "see me after work."
   Ⓓ "No, I don't," replied Anna.

6. Ⓐ My birthday is in June.
   Ⓑ Turn off the radio.
   Ⓒ He read from *The News Dispatch*.
   Ⓓ Sharon prefers doctor Ogata.

Darken the circle by the sentence in which capital letters are used correctly.

7. Ⓐ Do you know Dr. Gonzalez, janet?
   Ⓑ The german tourists were friendly.
   Ⓒ Pat said, "please come soon."
   Ⓓ He met Mayor Winston today.

8. Ⓐ My dear barbara,
   Ⓑ Sincerely Yours,
   Ⓒ Fairmont, VA 30097
   Ⓓ 322 w. Laroche St.

Darken the circle by the sentence in which end punctuation is used correctly.

9. Ⓐ I've never had such a great time?
   Ⓑ Did you know there's a blizzard outside.
   Ⓒ I came by to see how you are feeling!
   Ⓓ I don't know where my sock is.

10. Ⓐ Please don't go alone.
    Ⓑ Why are you here!
    Ⓒ Can you imagine what happened.
    Ⓓ Did he say anything else!

Darken the circle by the sentence in which the colon is used correctly.

11. Ⓐ Will you be done: by 100?
    Ⓑ I woke up at: 730.
    Ⓒ Bring these: items socks, shoes, and food.
    Ⓓ Before 4:30, it was bright and sunny.

12. Ⓐ Dear Ms. Phelps:
    Ⓑ My Dear Aunt:
    Ⓒ Yours truly:
    Ⓓ 635: P.M.

Darken the circle by the sentence in which the hyphen is used correctly.

13. Ⓐ I saw a beautiful-blue green fish.
    Ⓑ Dan and Christine have always cele-
       brated their birthdays together.
    Ⓒ My grandmother is ninety two-years old.

14. Ⓐ The second story-window is broken, and it
       needs to be fixed soon.
    Ⓑ My sister in-law lives in Toronto, Ontario.
    Ⓒ Her new puppy is well-behaved.

Language: Usage and Practice 7, SV 1419027840

Unit 4 Test, p. 2

Darken the circle by the sentence in which commas are used correctly.

15. Ⓐ "I can't go today, Sam" Alton said.

    Ⓑ After fishing we ate, swam and relaxed.

    Ⓒ Chad wants to go but, Todd can't.

    Ⓓ Dan, my neighbor, said he will meet us.

16. Ⓐ Oh I know I can do it, if I try.

    Ⓑ Jim told us "Be careful, not to slip!"

    Ⓒ Did you use sugar, cinnamon, and nutmeg?

    Ⓓ I called but, you weren't home.

17. Ⓐ Jeremy can you go, or not?

    Ⓑ Once she learns, Kaele will teach me to ski.

    Ⓒ Well I guess I'll go, now.

    Ⓓ My oldest friend Andrew, moved to Houston.

18. Ⓐ Cara asked, "How can you tell?"

    Ⓑ First I measured and then, I cut.

    Ⓒ How old are, you Maria?

    Ⓓ Since it rained we wrote letters, and read.

19. Ⓐ Yes, it's a good thing, we found out.

    Ⓑ "No" said Juan, "I don't want any."

    Ⓒ He lives in New Orleans, Louisiana.

    Ⓓ Who is the one, who did this?

20. Ⓐ Men, women and children are invited.

    Ⓑ A good neighbor's, Ted Barnes, house was flooded.

    Ⓒ Michael asked "What happened here?"

    Ⓓ We went first, and they followed shortly after.

Darken the circle by the sentence in which quotation marks are used incorrectly.

21. Ⓐ "When," asked Joseph, "are you leaving?"

    Ⓑ Sara told Scott, "I passed the test!"

    Ⓒ "Tell me when to stop," said Mary.

    Ⓓ "Gunnar added, I would never do that!"

22. Ⓐ "I can't believe the time! exclaimed Bert.

    Ⓑ Pablo asked, "Where are you going to dinner?"

    Ⓒ "Now," said Kayla, "we can relax."

    Ⓓ "I'm going to sit outside and read," said Sara.

23. Ⓐ "Wait for me!" cried Jake.

    Ⓑ Pedro said, "I can see for miles."

    Ⓒ "Well, said Ellen, it's not what I had imagined."

    Ⓓ "Do you think it will storm?" asked Holly.

24. Ⓐ "Don't worry," said Manuel. Everything is fine."

    Ⓑ "Let me tell you what I saw," said Joe.

    Ⓒ Laura asked, "What time should we meet?"

    Ⓓ "Brett," said Louis, "bring in the lawn chairs."

25. Ⓐ Roger said, "Nobody ever does what I ask."

    Ⓑ My friend, said Ross, "it's been a good year."

    Ⓒ "Let's look at houses," said Jalia.

    Ⓓ "Wait until you see the view!" said Rod.

26. Ⓐ "Show me which way they went," said Michelle.

    Ⓑ "Since you left," said Bill, "things are not the same."

    Ⓒ Belinda said, "I voted for Judge Jackson."

    Ⓓ "Doug said, He didn't want to go to Minneapolis, Minnesota."

Darken the circle by the sentence that needs an apostrophe.

27. Ⓐ Our dogs fur is thicker in winter.

    Ⓑ Your gloves are in the car.

    Ⓒ Our neighbors bought a dog.

    Ⓓ Sheena brought home two loaves of bread.

28. Ⓐ The copies she made were difficult to read.

    Ⓑ Club members must volunteer ten hours a week.

    Ⓒ The childrens poems were the hit of the talent show.

    Ⓓ Two rooms must be reserved for the party.

    Language: Usage and Practice 7, SV 1419027840

Writing Sentences

- Every sentence has a base consisting of a simple subject and a simple predicate.
  EXAMPLE: Amanda baked.
- Expand the meaning of a sentence by adding adjectives, adverbs, and prepositional phrases to the sentence base.
  EXAMPLE: **My cousin** Amanda baked **a delicious orange cake for dessert.**

 Expand the meaning of each sentence base by adding adjectives, adverbs, and/or prepositional phrases. Write each expanded sentence below.

1. (Carl swam.)

   _____

2. (Clock ticked.)

   _____

3. (Snow falls.)

   _____

4. (Sun rose.)

   _____

5. (Fireworks exploded.)

   _____

Imagine two different scenes for each sentence base below. Write an expanded sentence to describe each scene you imagine.

6. (Students listened.)   **a.** _____

   b. _____

7. (Jason wrote.)   **a.** _____

   b. _____

8. (Kamal played.)   **a.** _____

   b. _____

9. (Juan drove.)   **a.** _____

   b. _____

10. (We helped.)   **a.** _____

   b. _____

Name _____ Date _____

Writing Topic Sentences

- A **topic sentence** states the main idea of a paragraph.
- It is often placed at the beginning of a paragraph.
  EXAMPLE:
  Mario was asked to write an article about the new recreation center for the school paper. He wrote a list of questions to ask. He interviewed the park superintendent. He found out about the old park and why it was necessary to build a recreation center.

 Underline the topic sentence in each paragraph below.

1. Mario knew that having good questions was very important to a successful interview. He thought carefully about what he wanted to know. Then he divided his questions into groups. Some were about the building. Some were about recreation. Others were about the staff.

2. He wanted to include something about the history of the park. He found out who first owned the land. He also asked how people had used the park over the years.

3. Mario found out that the park was nearly as old as the town itself. It had been the scene of picnics, baseball games, carnivals, concerts, and holiday festivals. Political meetings had also been held there.

 Write a topic sentence for each group of sentences below.

4. Topic Sentence: _____
   a. Jim Leland was the park superintendent.
   b. He had worked in the field of recreation and sports all his adult life.
   c. His father had been a high-school teacher and coach.
   d. His grandfather had been a popular baseball player.

5. Topic Sentence: _____
   a. Mario enjoyed talking to Jim.
   b. He found out more than he had ever expected.
   c. Jim told him why the community needed the center.
   d. The city had grown, and it needed to provide recreation for its residents.

 Think of a topic you are interested in. Write the topic on the line. Then write a topic sentence.

Topic: _____

Topic Sentence: _____

_____

Writing Supporting Details

- The idea expressed in the topic sentence can be developed with sentences containing **supporting details**.
- Details can include facts, examples, and reasons.

 Circle the topic sentence and underline only the sentences containing supporting details in the paragraph below.

Mario asked Theresa to help him with the article. She would write out the tape-recorded interviews. She would also make suggestions for changes. Theresa is very athletic. Finally, they would both work on typing the article.

 After each topic sentence, write five sentences containing supporting details.

1. You must be organized when writing an article.

a. _____

b. _____

c. _____

d. _____

e. _____

2. It is important to learn all you can about your topic.

a. _____

b. _____

c. _____

d. _____

e. _____

 Write four sentences that contain supporting details for the topic sentence you wrote at the bottom of page 94.

Topic Sentence: _____

a. _____

b. _____

c. _____

d. _____

e. _____

Language: Usage and Practice 7, SV 1419027840

Ordering Information Within a Paragraph

- One way to organize information in a paragraph is to put it in **chronological order**—the time in which events occurred.
- Words such as <u>first</u>, <u>next</u>, <u>second</u>, <u>then</u>, <u>finally</u>, and <u>later</u> are used to indicate the order in which events happen.
  EXAMPLE: **First**, Mario checked his tape recorder. **Then**, he left for the interview.
- Another way to organize information is to use **spatial order**.
- Words such as <u>above</u>, <u>near</u>, <u>over</u>, <u>beside</u>, <u>right</u>, <u>left</u>, <u>closer</u>, <u>farther</u>, <u>up</u>, and <u>down</u> are used to express spatial relationships.
  EXAMPLE: The bald eagle sat on **top** of the tree. He watched the pond **below**.

 Read each paragraph below and tell whether it is in chronological order or spatial order. For the paragraph in chronological order, underline the time order words. For the paragraph in spatial order, underline the words that indicate spatial order.

1.   The park board of directors must first approve the architect's design for the recreation center. Then, they must develop and approve a budget for the construction of the center. Finally, they can give approval to construction of the center.

  Order: _____

2.   The plan for the recreation center includes play areas for young children. A slide and swing set will be built next to a large sandbox. A jungle gym will be to the left of the slide. Children will be able to climb to the top of the jungle gym and then jump down to the ground.

  Order: _____

Number the details below in chronological order.

3. _____ Then, early in March, the park board of directors approved the architect's design.

  _____ Next, the budget was approved in April.

  _____ The center's roof was finally completed in August.

  _____ In January, the architect finished his design.

Choose one of the scenes below. Write a paragraph of at least four sentences describing the scene. Use spatial order words to show location.

  Scenes: your house, a ballpark, a restaurant, a theater, a friend's house

_____

_____

_____

_____

Topic and Audience

> • The **topic** of a story or an article is the subject written about.
> • The **audience** is the group of readers.
>   EXAMPLES: students, family members, neighbors, readers of a newspaper

✳ **Choose the most likely audience for each topic listed below.**

a. first graders   **b.** the city council   **c.** high school students   **d.** parents

_____ 1. Star Athlete Visits Students at Recreation Center

_____ 2. Study Shows Connection between Time Spent Exercising and Student Progress in School

_____ 3. Peter Rabbit Here for Hop and Jump Exercises

_____ 4. Council Considers Tax Plans to Finance Recreation Center

_____ 5. Tryouts for High School Track Team on Friday

_____ 6. Study Shows City Budget Shortfall Next Year

_____ 7. Kelsey School Parents' Night Next Thursday

_____ 8. Officer Safety to Visit Young Students Next Week

_____ 9. State University Considers Raising Tuition

_____ 10. Governor Approves Funds to Expand City Bus Service

✳ **Read the paragraph below. Then answer the questions that follow.**

On Tuesday evening, May 2, 2007, at 6:00, Hawkeye, the mascot of the Child Protection Foundation, will be at the park with his handler, Officer Roy Meyers. While Hawkeye, the long-eared hound, entertains the youngsters, Officer Meyers will discuss the topic "Keeping Your Children Safe." This unusual pair has traveled across the state to introduce the findings on topics such as accidents in the home, hazardous toys, and bike safety.

11. What is the topic of the paragraph?

_____

12. Name two possible audiences for the paragraph.

_____

13. Explain why each audience might be interested.

Audience 1: _____

Audience 2: _____

✳ **Choose a topic in which you are interested. Write the name of the topic and name the audience it would be most likely to interest.**

Topic: _____

Audience: _____

Clustering

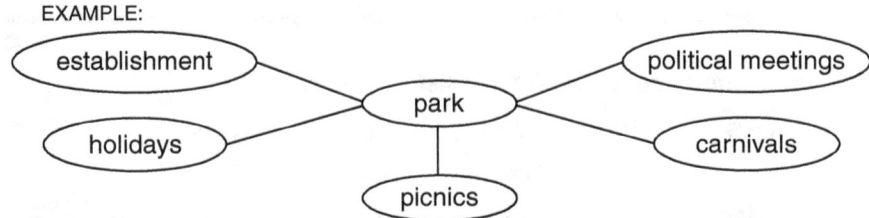

- A **clustering diagram** shows how ideas relate to a particular topic.
- The topic is written in the center. Related ideas are written around the topic.
- Lines show the connections between the ideas.

EXAMPLE:

establishment — park — political meetings
holidays — park — carnivals
picnics

Topic Sentence: The recreation center will be built on land that was once a park.

 Read each paragraph below. Notice the underlined topic sentence as you read. Then fill in each cluster to show how the details relating to that topic sentence could have been chosen.

1. Mario had a great deal of work to do for the article. He had to finish the interviews, decide what information to use, and write a rough draft. He then had to revise the draft, type the final copy, and proofread it.

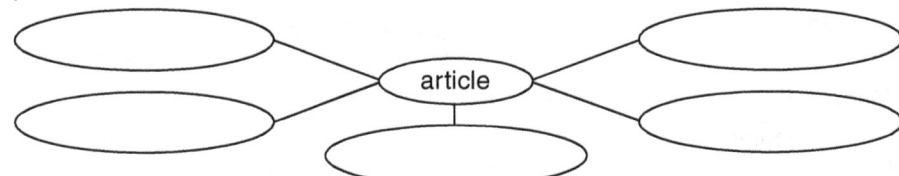

article

2. Theresa worked hard on the article. She typed the interviews. She edited the article. She organized the rough draft. Finally, she helped with the final revision and proofreading.

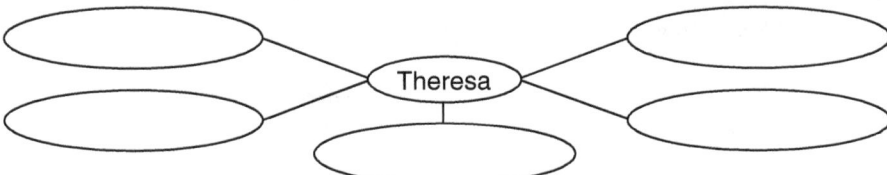

Theresa

 Rewrite the topic sentence you wrote at the bottom of page 94.

Topic Sentence: _____

 Write the topic you wrote at the bottom of page 94 in the center of the cluster below. Then fill in the cluster with details that would support your main topic.

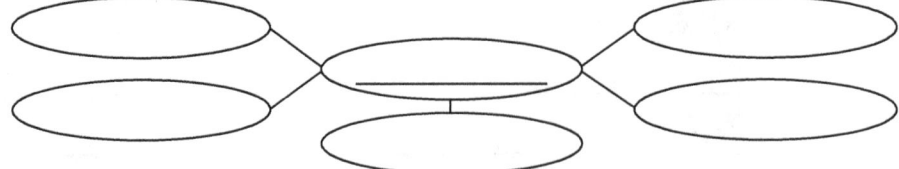

Outlining

- Before you write about a topic, organize your thoughts by making an **outline**.
- An outline consists of the **title** of the topic, **main headings** for the main ideas, and **subheadings** for supporting ideas.
- Main headings are listed after Roman numerals. Subheadings are listed after capital letters.

Topic: The need for a recreation center

I. Problems with park
 A. Age of equipment
 B. Limited usefulness for residents
II. Advantages of recreation center
 A. Wide range of uses
 B. Safe, up-to-date equipment

 Refer to your topic sentence and cluster at the bottom of page 98. Write an outline based on the cluster, using the example outline as a guide.

Topic: _____

I. _____

    A. _____

    B. _____

II. _____

    A. _____

    B. _____

III. _____

    A. _____

    B. _____

IV. _____

    A. _____

    B. _____

V. _____

    A. _____

    B. _____

Language: Usage and Practice 7, SV 1419027840

Preparing Interview Questions

- Writers use **interviews** to get information.
- Good interview questions will encourage the person being interviewed to talk freely about the subject.
  - EXAMPLES: Why do we need a recreation center?
  - Who will be involved in making decisions?
- Avoid questions that can be answered either <u>yes</u> or <u>no</u> by beginning them with words such as <u>who</u>, <u>what</u>, <u>why</u>, and <u>how</u>.
  - EXAMPLE: Why do we need a recreation center?

✳ **Write <u>who</u>, <u>what</u>, <u>when</u>, <u>where</u>, <u>why</u>, or <u>how</u> to complete each question.**

1. _____ will vote on the budget for the recreation center?

2. _____ will be the various uses of the center?

3. _____ will the center be paid for?

4. _____ will the center be located?

5. _____ do you think a recreation center is necessary?

6. _____ will the center be completed?

✳ **Rewrite the questions below so that they cannot be answered <u>yes</u> or <u>no</u>.**

7. Does the park have an interesting history?

_____

8. Is the location of the park good?

_____

9. Does the council have plans to raise local taxes?

_____

10. Will the townspeople have a say on the new recreation center?

_____

✳ **Choose a topic and write three questions about it. Remember to begin each question with <u>who</u>, <u>what</u>, <u>when</u>, <u>where</u>, <u>why</u>, or <u>how</u>.**

Topic: _____

11. _____

12. _____

13. _____

Writing Based on an Interview

> - Many factual articles are based on information gathered in an interview.
> - The writer asks questions about the subject he or she wants to cover and then uses the information to write an article.

 Read the notes from the interview. Then read the paragraph that Mario and Theresa wrote and answer the questions that follow.

Question 1: Jim, how do you feel about the proposed recreation center?

Answer: It is definitely needed. The park is too small for our growing city and needs massive repairs anyway. It will be good for the whole city to have a well-equipped recreation center.

Question 2: Your family has been involved in sports for many years. How do you feel about the modern approach to physical fitness for people of all ages?

Answer: Physical fitness is vital for everyone. That's why the new recreation center is so important. It will offer facilities and programs for everyone, regardless of age or current fitness level.

Question 3: What will the recreation center include?

Answer: The center will house an indoor pool, a small ice rink, two gyms, meeting rooms, arts-and-crafts facilities, and locker rooms with showers. We also hope to include a weight-lifting room.

> According to Mr. Jim Leland, park superintendent, the new recreation center will be a welcome addition to the city's facilities. The old park is now outdated and can no longer fill the needs of the people. Mr. Leland recommends that the park be the site of the new recreation center. Its facilities, which will include an indoor pool and two gyms, will fit everyone's needs, regardless of age or current fitness level.

1. Does the author quote Mr. Leland exactly? _____

2. Write one sentence in the article that came from question 1.

_____

3. Write one sentence in the article that came from question 3.

_____

4. Write another question that Mario could have asked Mr. Leland.

_____

5. What other things will the recreation center include that were not in the article?

_____

Language: Usage and Practice 7, SV 1419027840

Revising and Proofreading

- **Revising** gives you a chance to rethink and review what you have written and to improve your writing. Revise by adding words and information, by taking out unneeded words and information, and by moving words, sentences, and paragraphs around.
- **Proofreading** has to do with checking spelling, punctuation, grammar, and capitalization. Use proofreader's marks to show changes needed in your writing.

Proofreader's Marks

=	⊙	(SP)
Capitalize.	Add a period.	Correct spelling.
/	∧	¶
Make a small letter.	Add something.	Indent for new paragraph.
⋏	℘	⌒
Add a comma.	Take something out.	Move something.

Rewrite the paragraph below. Correct the errors by following the proofreader's marks.

¶ The berryton city council today appruved plans today for construction of a New recreation center mayor june booth said the center to be located on the sight of the currant adams park will provide berryton residents with a variety of recreational programs" the center's facilities include will an indoor pool to gymnasiums arts-and-crafts facilities and a small ice rink and an indoor pool Several meating rooms will also be Included too for use buy various organizations.

_____

_____

_____

_____

_____

_____

_____

_____

Revising and Proofreading, p. 2

 Read the paragraphs below. Use proofreader's marks to revise and proofread the paragraphs. Then write your revised paragraphs below.

Representatives from severals community organizations attended the meeting to express their support of the recreation center. "Construction of this center is Long Overdue Are members will now have a central place in which to meat instead of crowding into each other's homes said Milton Sayre chairman of the berryton citizens senior league

plans call for a groundbreaking ceremony on thursday may 16 at 2 30 followed by a reception in adams park Construction is scheduled mayor booth superintendent jim leland and city council members will participate all residents are invited to join them at the ceremoney

_____

_____

_____

_____

_____

_____

_____

_____

_____

_____

_____

_____

_____

Unit 5 Test

Read the paragraph. Then darken the circle by the correct answer to each question.

Many Moroccans dress in very traditional clothing, wearing long robes and veils or turbans. Others wear modern Western clothing. Several languages are spoken in Morocco, including Arabic, Berber, French, and Spanish. Morocco's landscape is nearly as varied as the cultures that have influenced its people. You can find barren deserts, fertile farmlands, forested mountains, and sandy beaches all within this northwestern region of Africa.

1. Which sentence could best be used as a topic sentence for the paragraph above?

Ⓐ Morocco's official language is Arabic.

Ⓑ Morocco has many interesting sights and sounds.

Ⓒ Many languages are spoken in Morocco.

Ⓓ Morocco has a beautiful landscape.

2. Which sentence would add the most appropriate supporting detail to the paragraph above?

Ⓐ My brother wants to go to Morocco.

Ⓑ Spanish is also spoken in Mexico.

Ⓒ A popular Moroccan dish is called couscous.

Ⓓ You can see the French and Spanish influences in Moroccan art.

3. Which audience would be the most interested in this paragraph?

Ⓐ football players

Ⓑ waitresses

Ⓒ preschool children

Ⓓ travelers

Darken the circle by the correct answer to each question.

4. Which word does not indicate chronological order?

Ⓐ finally   Ⓒ around

Ⓑ next   Ⓓ then

5. Which sentence would come first in chronological order?

Ⓐ By February, the ground was frozen solid.

Ⓑ The fall was uncommonly cold.

Ⓒ At the end of the year, snow began piling up.

Ⓓ Cold weather kept many travelers at home.

6. Which is not a way of organizing information or ideas?

Ⓐ clustering   Ⓒ interviewing

Ⓑ chronological order   Ⓓ outlining

7. Which word indicates spatial order?

Ⓐ nearly   Ⓒ region

Ⓑ within   Ⓓ landscape

8. Which sentence does not use spatial order?

Ⓐ The only phone booth is around the corner.

Ⓑ Go down the street a block and then turn left.

Ⓒ You will find a telephone book inside the booth.

Ⓓ Use it to look up the number of the station.

9. Which is not part of an outline?

Ⓐ headings   Ⓒ audience

Ⓑ title   Ⓓ subheadings

Unit 5 Test, p. 2

Darken the circle by the correct answer to each question.

10. Which is the best interview question?

    (A) Will the city's orchestra do as well this year?

    (B) Do you enjoy singing in front of a crowd?

    (C) Are there any new goals for your company?

    (D) Why did you decide to run for office?

11. Which word is not good for an interview question?

    (A) how

    (B) where

    (C) does

    (D) who

Read the outline below. Then darken the circle by the correct answers to the questions that follow.

Topic: Staying safe in your home

  I. When you're at home
    A. Keep doors and windows locked
    B. Close shades or curtains at night
    C. _____

  II. _____
    A. Leave lights on inside and outside
    B. Leave a radio on

12. Which fits best in subhead C?

    (A) Don't answer the telephone

    (B) Don't open the door to a stranger

    (C) Don't watch television

    (D) Don't leave your car outside

13. Which fits best in head II?

    (A) When you're away from home

    (B) Lighting your home

    (C) Keeping people away

    (D) How dogs guard homes

Darken the circle by the correct revision of each underlined sentence.

14. After the Pinskes called mr. an Mrs. Fisk then for left the airport.

    (A) The Pinskes called, after Dr. and Mrs. Fisk Then left for the airport.

    (B) After the Pinskes calld. Mr. an Mrs. Fisk left for the airport.

    (C) After the Pinskes called, Mr. and Mrs. Fisk left for the airport.

    (D) The pinskes called and Dr. and Mrs. Fist left for the airport.

15. many peple visit wyoming not very many live there actually

    (A) Although many people visit Wyoming, not very many live there.

    (B) Many people visit Wyoming but actually not very many live there.

    (C) Although people visit Wyoming, actually not many people live there.

    (D) Although many people visit Wyoming, not very many actually live there.

Darken the circle by the sentence that shows the correct proofreader's marks for the revised numbered sentence.

16. In order to work with our program, please complete the attached application.

    (A) in order to to work with our Program please compleat the attached application.

    (B) To work with our program, attach a completed aplication.

    (C) In order work with the program, please attach a application.

    (D) in order to work with our pogram please complete the applicaton.

     Language: Usage and Practice 7, SV 1419027840

Dictionary: Guide Words

- A **dictionary** is a reference book that contains definitions of words and other information about their history and use.
- **Entries** in a dictionary are listed in **alphabetical order**.
- **Guide words** appear at the top of each dictionary page. Guide words show the first and last entry on the page.
  EXAMPLE: The word <u>lease</u> would appear on a dictionary page with the guide words <u>learn</u> / <u>lesson</u>. The word <u>lever</u> would not.

 Put a check in front of each word that would be listed on a dictionary page with the given guide words.

1. fade / flat	2. image / inform	3. radio / reach
_____ faster	_____ information	_____ rail
_____ face	_____ impossible	_____ rabbit
_____ flavor	_____ insect	_____ ranch
_____ fetch	_____ incomplete	_____ real
_____ flatter	_____ ignore	_____ raw
_____ factory	_____ immense	_____ raccoon
_____ flag	_____ indeed	_____ raft
_____ fancy	_____ improve	_____ read
_____ flop	_____ insist	_____ ramp
_____ fertile	_____ infect	_____ rate
_____ flow	_____ imagine	_____ reduce
_____ flame	_____ inherit	_____ rake

Number the words in each column in the order of their appearance in a dictionary. Then write the words that could be the guide words for each column.

4. _____ / _____	5. _____ / _____	6. _____ / _____
_____ bedroom	_____ dine	_____ fire
_____ blend	_____ depend	_____ face
_____ blame	_____ determine	_____ free
_____ biography	_____ department	_____ finger
_____ block	_____ district	_____ faint
_____ blink	_____ disease	_____ flower
_____ bear	_____ disturb	_____ family
_____ benefit	_____ discard	_____ follow
_____ believe	_____ difference	_____ fair
_____ beach	_____ dessert	_____ flavor

Name _____ Date _____

Dictionary: Syllables

- A **syllable** is a part of a word that is pronounced at one time.
- Dictionary entry words are divided into syllables to show how they can be divided at the end of a writing line.
- A **hyphen (-)** is placed between syllables to separate them.
  EXAMPLE: quar-ter-back
- If a word has a beginning or ending syllable of only one letter, do not divide it at the end of a writing line so that one letter stands alone.
  EXAMPLES: a-fraid   bus-y

✳ **Find each word in a dictionary. Then write each word with a hyphen between each syllable.**

1. allowance _____
2. porridge _____
3. harness _____
4. peddle _____
5. character _____
6. hickory _____
7. solution _____
8. variety _____
9. talent _____
10. weather _____

11. brilliant _____
12. enthusiasm _____
13. dramatic _____
14. employment _____
15. laboratory _____
16. judgment _____
17. kingdom _____
18. recognize _____
19. usual _____
20. yesterday _____

✳ **Write two ways in which each word may be divided at the end of a writing line.**

21. victorious   vic-torious   victori-ous
22. inferior _____   _____
23. quantity _____   _____
24. satisfactory _____   _____
25. security _____   _____
26. possession _____   _____
27. thermometer _____   _____
28. getaway _____   _____

Name _____ Date _____

Dictionary: Definitions and Parts of Speech

- A dictionary lists the **definitions** of each entry word. Many words have more than one definition. In this case, the most commonly used definition is given first. Sometimes a definition is followed by a sentence showing a use of the entry word.
- A dictionary also gives the **part of speech** for each entry word. An abbreviation (shown below) stands for each part of speech. Some words may be used as more than one part of speech.
  EXAMPLE: **mess** (mes) *n.* **1.** an untidy, usually dirty, condition. *-v.* to make untidy and dirty.

 Use the dictionary samples below to answer the questions.

cage (kāj) *n.* a structure in which animals can be kept. *-v.* to lock up or keep in a cage.

cos-tume (kos´ tōōm) *n.* **1.** an outfit worn in pretending to be someone else: *Karla's costume was the nicest one in the play.* **2.** a type of dress associated with a particular people, place, or time. *-v.* to provide with a costume.

cot-ton (kot´ ən) *n.* **1.** soft fibers that grow in a cluster on seed pods of certain plants and are used to make cloth. **2.** the plant on which these fibers grow. **3.** thread made from cotton fibers. **4.** cloth woven of cotton. *-adj.* made of cotton: *The cotton dress might shrink in warm water.*

1. Which words can be used as either a noun

   or a verb? _____

2. Which word can be used as an adjective?

   _____

n.	noun
pron.	pronoun
v.	verb
adj.	adjective
adv.	adverb
prep.	preposition

3. Which word has the most meanings?

   _____

4. Which word can be used as a noun or as an adjective? _____

5. Write the most commonly used definition of costume. _____

   _____

6. Write a sentence in which you use cage as a verb. _____

   _____

7. Write a sentence using the first definition of costume. _____

   _____

8. Use the second definition of cotton in a sentence. _____

   _____

Language: Usage and Practice 7, SV 1419027840

Dictionary: Word Origins

- An **etymology** tells of an entry word's origin and development. Many dictionary entries include an etymology.
- The etymology is usually enclosed in brackets [ ] after the definition of the entry word. The language from which the entry word came into English is listed first, followed by the language from which that word came, and so on.
- Often the symbol ≤ is used to save space and stands for the phrase "is derived from" or "comes from."

    EXAMPLE: **tu-lip** (too′ lip, tyoo′ lip) [Lat. *Tulipa* < Turk. *tülibend*, turban < Pers. *dulband*] The word *tulip* came into English from the New Latin word *Tulipa*, which came from the Turkish word *tülibend*, which meant "turban." The word *tülibend* came from the Persian word *dulband*.

 Use the dictionary samples below to answer the questions.

e-mo-tion (i mō′ shən) *n.* strong feeling. [Middle French *emouvoir* to stir up, from Latin *exmovēre* to move away, disturb from *ex* + *movēre* to move]

gup-py (gup′ ē) *n.* a small, brightly colored freshwater fish. [After R. J. L. Guppy (1836–1916), who introduced the fish to England]

line (līn) *n.* a long, narrow mark as with pen or pencil. [A combination of Old French *ligne* string, cord and Old English *line* cord, rope]

load (lōd) *n.* **1.** that which is put on a pack animal to carry. **2.** cargo put on a ship, plane, train, or truck. [Middle English *lod*, from Old English *lād* support, carrying]

mar-a-thon (mar′ a thon′) *n.* a cross-country foot race. [After *Marathon*, Greece (so called because in 490 B.C. a messenger ran from Marathon to Athens to announce a victory over the Persians)]

1. Which word comes from the name of a person? _____

2. Which word originally meant "to move"? _____

3. Which languages are in the history of the word line? _____

4. Which word comes from both Middle English and Old English? _____

5. Which word comes from the name of a place? _____

6. Which words have more than one language in their histories? _____

7. What is the meaning of the Latin word exmovēre? _____

8. Why is the guppy named after R. J. L. Guppy? _____

9. What did the Middle English word lod come from? _____

10. Why do we call a long race a marathon? _____

_____

11. Which word comes from a word that meant "support or carrying"? _____

12. Which word comes from the word ligne? _____

13. Which words come from French? _____

Using Parts of a Book

- A **title page** lists the name of a book and its author.
- A **copyright page** tells who published the book, where it was published, and when it was published.
- A **table of contents** lists the chapter or unit titles and the page numbers on which they begin. It is at the front of a book.
- An **index** gives a detailed list of the topics in a book and the page numbers on which each topic is found. It is in the back of a book.

 Answer the questions below.

1. Where should you look for the page number of a particular topic? _____

2. Where should you look to find out who wrote a book? _____

3. Where should you look to get a general idea of the contents of a book? _____

4. Where should you look to find out when a book was published? _____

5. Where should you look to find the name of the book? _____

6. Where should you look to find out who published a book? _____

Use the table of contents below to answer the questions.

7. What is this book about? _____

8. On what pages can you read about the tribe and its ways? _____

9. On what pages can you read about war and defeat? _____

10. On what pages can you read about appearance? _____

11. What can you read about on pages 10–13? _____

12. What can you read about on pages 28–29? _____

13. Does the book contain a glossary? _____

14. Where is the index located? _____

Name _____ Date _____

Using the Library

> - Nonfiction books on library shelves are arranged by **call numbers**.
> - Each book is assigned a number from 000 to 999, according to its subject matter.
> - The main subject groups for call numbers are as follows:
>
>   000–099 Reference   500–599 Science and Math
>   100–199 Philosophy   600–699 Technology
>   200–299 Religion   700–799 The Arts
>   300–399 Social Sciences   800–899 Literature
>   400–499 Languages   900–999 History and Geography

✳ **Write the call number group in which you would find each book.**

1. *World Almanac and Book of Facts* _____

2. *Mathematics for Today* _____

3. *Global Warming: A World Problem* _____

4. *Philosophy Through the Ages* _____

5. *Spanish: A Romance Language* _____

6. *Technology Takes Over* _____

7. *Splitting the Atom* _____

8. *The Encyclopedia of Mammals* _____

9. *The Impressionist School of Painting* _____

10. *Children's Stories from Around the World* _____

11. *The Study of Forgotten Societies* _____

12. *The New Russia* _____

13. *The Religions of the World* _____

14. *The Readers' Guide* _____

15. *Dance in North America* _____

✳ **Write the titles of three of your favorite nonfiction books. Write the call number range beside each title.**

16. _____

17. _____

18. _____

     Language: Usage and Practice 7, SV 1419027840

Using an Encyclopedia

- An **encyclopedia** is a reference book that contains articles on many different topics.
- The articles are arranged alphabetically in volumes. Each volume is marked to show which articles are inside.
- Guide words are used to show the first topic on each page.
- At the end of most articles, there is a listing of cross-references to related topics for the reader to investigate.

Find the entry for <u>Knute Rockne</u> in an encyclopedia. Then answer the following questions.

1. Which encyclopedia did you use? _____

2. When did Knute Rockne live? _____

3. Where was he born? _____

4. Where did he go to college? _____

5. For what is he best known? _____

Find the entry for <u>Redwood</u> in an encyclopedia. Then answer the following questions.

6. Which encyclopedia did you use? _____

7. Where does the redwood tree grow?_____

8. By what other name is it known? _____

9. What is special about this tree? _____

10. How tall do most redwoods grow? _____

Find the entry in an encyclopedia for a person in whom you are interested. Then answer the following questions.

11. Who is your subject? _____

12. Which encyclopedia did you use? _____

13. When did the person live? _____

14. Where did the person live? _____

15. What is it about the person that makes him or her famous? _____

16. What cross-references are listed? _____

Name _____ Date _____

Using an Encyclopedia Index

- Most encyclopedias have an **index** of subject titles, listed in alphabetical order.
- The index shows the volume and the page number where an article can be found.
- Some encyclopedias contain articles on many different topics. Other encyclopedias contain different articles relating to a broad general topic.

 Use the sample encyclopedia index to answer the questions below.

> **Index**
> **Acorn Squash**, 1–6; **11**–1759
>   Baked, supreme, **1**–7
>   Steamed, **1**–7
> **Appetizer(s)**, 1–841; *see also* Cocktail; Dip; Pickle and Relish; Spread
>   Almonds, **1**–89
>   Celery, stuffed, **1**–89
>   Cheese Ball, **3**–429
> **Cabbage**, 2–256; *see also* Salads, Coleslaw; Sauerkraut
> with bacon and cheese sauce, **1**–68
> **Flour**, 5–705
>   Peanut, **8**–1328
>   Rice, **10**–1556
>   Wheat, **12**–1935

1. In which volume would you find an article on stuffed celery? _____

2. On which page would you find information on cabbage with bacon and cheese sauce? _____

3. Are all articles on flour found in the same volume? _____

4. What are the cross-references for **Appetizers**? _____

5. Do the words in bold show the name of the volume or the name of the main food or ingredient? _____

6. Which main food or ingredient has articles in two volumes? _____

7. Information on which appetizers can be found in the same volume and on the same page? _____

_____

8. Which main ingredient is found in Volume 5? _____

9. If you looked under **Dip**, what might you expect to find as a cross-reference? _____

_____

10. Information on which appetizer would be found in Volume 3? _____

11. Information on which ingredient is found on page 1328 in the encyclopedia? _____

    Language: Usage and Practice 7, SV 1419027840

Using the *Readers' Guide*

- The ***Readers' Guide to Periodical Literature*** lists by author and by subject all the articles that appear in nearly two hundred magazines.

Use the *Readers' Guide* when you need

- Recent articles on a particular subject,
- Several articles written over a period of time about the same subject,
- Many articles written by the same author.

 Use the *Readers' Guide* samples to answer the questions.

Subject Entry

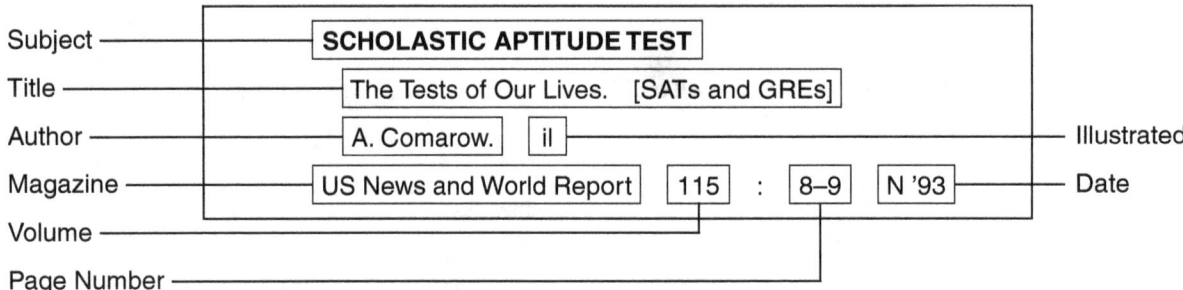

Subject — SCHOLASTIC APTITUDE TEST
Title — The Tests of Our Lives. [SATs and GREs]
Author — A. Comarow. il — Illustrated
Magazine — US News and World Report 115 : 8–9 N '93 — Date
Volume
Page Number

Author Entry

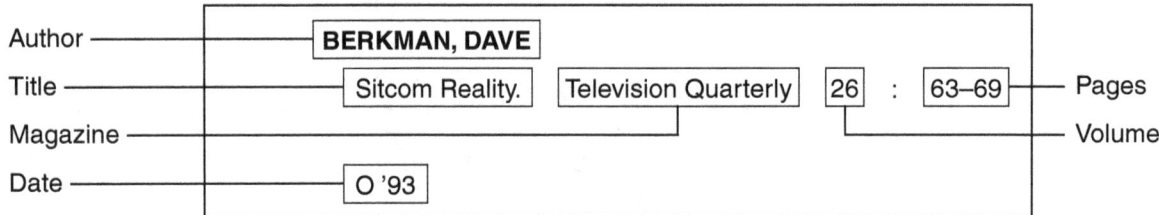

Author — BERKMAN, DAVE
Title — Sitcom Reality. Television Quarterly 26 : 63–69 — Pages
Magazine — Volume
Date — O '93

1. Who wrote the article "Sitcom Reality"? _____

2. In which magazine will you find the article "The Tests of Our Lives"? _____

3. Who is the author of "The Tests of Our Lives"? _____

4. In which magazine will you find the article "Sitcom Reality"? _____

5. Under what subject entry might you find the article "Sitcom Reality"? _____

6. On what pages will you find the article "Sitcom Reality"? _____

7. In which volume of *US News and World Report* does "The Tests of Our Lives" appear? _____

8. In which month and year was "The Tests of Our Lives" published? _____

9. What abbreviation is used for the word <u>illustrated</u>? _____

10. In what month and year was "Sitcom Reality" published? _____

Name _____   Date _____

Choosing Reference Sources

- Use a **dictionary** to find the definitions of words and pronunciations of words, suggestions for word usage, and etymologies.
- Use an **encyclopedia** to find articles about many different people, places, and other subjects. Use an encyclopedia to find references to related subjects.
- Use a **thesaurus** to find synonyms and antonyms.
- Use the *Readers' Guide to Periodical Literature* to find magazine articles on specific subjects or by particular authors.
- Use an **atlas** to find maps and other information about geographical locations.
- Use an **almanac**, an annual publication, to find such information as population numbers, annual rainfall, election statistics, and other specific information for a given year.

Write dictionary, encyclopedia, thesaurus, *Readers' Guide*, atlas, or almanac to show where you would find the following information. Some information may be found in more than one source.

_____   **1.** the life of Queen Elizabeth I

_____   **2.** an article on the latest space shuttle flight

_____   **3.** the states and provinces through which the Rocky Mountains run

_____   **4.** the origin of the word tomato

_____   **5.** the annual rainfall for Somalia

_____   **6.** the most direct route from California to Alberta

_____   **7.** an antonym for the word happy

_____   **8.** the meaning of the word spar

_____   **9.** recent articles written on the subject of air pollution

_____   **10.** the pronunciation of the word wren

_____   **11.** the life of Sigmund Freud

_____   **12.** a synonym for the word bad

_____   **13.** the years during which World War I was fought

_____   **14.** an article on rock climbing

_____   **15.** the final standings of the National Football League for last year

_____   **16.** the meaning of the word history

Name _____ Date _____

Using Reference Sources

- Use reference sources—dictionaries, encyclopedias, the *Readers' Guide to Periodical Literature*, thesauruses, atlases, and almanacs—to find information about people, places, or things with which you are not familiar.
- You can also use these sources to find out more about subjects that interest you.

Follow the directions below.

1. Choose a person from history that you would like to know more about.

   Person's name: _____

2. Name two reference sources that you can use to find information about this person.

   a. _____

   b. _____

3. Use one of the reference sources you named above. Find the entry for the person you are researching. Write the exact title of the reference.

   _____

4. Write a short summary of the information you found.

   _____

   _____

   _____

   _____

5. Name the source that would contain recent articles about this person.

   _____

6. Look up your person's name in the reference source you listed in number 5. Write the titles of three articles that were listed.

   a. _____

   b. _____

   c. _____

7. Which articles above, if any, can be found in your library?

   _____

8. Name a subject heading under which you might find more information on your person.

   _____

Using Reference Sources, p. 2

 Follow the directions and answer the questions.

9. Choose a country you would like to know more about.

   Name of country: _____

10. List four reference sources that you can use to find information about this country.

   a. _____

   b. _____

   c. _____

   d. _____

11. Find the entry for the country in one of the reference sources you listed.
   Write the exact title of the reference source.

   _____

12. Write a short summary of the information you found. _____

   _____

   _____

   _____

13. Find the entry for the country in one other reference source. Write the exact title of the reference source.

   _____

14. What new information did you find about the country? _____

   _____

   _____

 **Follow the directions and answer the questions.**

15. In which state do you live? _____

16. Find the entry for your state in one of the reference sources. Write the exact title of the reference source.

   _____

17. Write a short summary of the information you found about your state. _____

   _____

   _____

   _____

Name _____   Date _____

Unit 6 Test

Refer to the dictionary samples to answer the questions that follow. Darken the circle by your choice.

lem-on (lem´ ən) *n.* **1.** a small, oval citrus fruit with a yellow rind and sour pulp. **2.** a bright yellow color. *-adj.* **1.** being the color lemon. **2.** made from lemon: *I used lemon juice on the fish.* [Middle English *lymon*, from Middle French *limon*]
load (lōd) *n.* **1.** something carried or to be carried in one trip. **2.** an amount that can be carried. **3.** something that

is a burden. *-v.* **1.** to place or put something. **2.** to supply abundantly. [Middle English *lode*, from Old English *lād*, a journey]
lob-ster (läb´ ster) *n.* **1.** an edible, saltwater sea animal with five pairs of legs, one of which has pincer claws. **2.** the flesh of this animal used for food: *Do you like lobster?*

1. Which word has only one syllable?

  Ⓐ load   Ⓑ lobster   Ⓒ lemon

2. Which word has the most definitions?

  Ⓐ load   Ⓑ lobster   Ⓒ lemon

3. Which word serves as only one part of speech?

  Ⓐ load   Ⓑ lobster   Ⓒ lemon

4. Which word is both a noun and an adjective?

  Ⓐ lobster   Ⓑ load   Ⓒ lemon

5. Which word originally meant "journey"?

  Ⓐ load   Ⓑ lobster   Ⓒ lemon

6. As which part of speech can load not be used?

  Ⓐ noun   Ⓑ verb   Ⓒ adjective

7. From how many other languages did lemon come?

  Ⓐ two   Ⓑ three   Ⓒ one

8. For which word is no etymology given?

  Ⓐ load   Ⓑ lobster   Ⓒ lemon

Darken the circle by the reference source you would use to find the following information.

9. an antonym for the word clever

  Ⓐ encyclopedia   Ⓒ *Readers' Guide*

  Ⓑ thesaurus   Ⓓ atlas

10. information on Quebec, Canada

  Ⓐ encyclopedia   Ⓒ *Readers' Guide*

  Ⓑ thesaurus   Ⓓ atlas

11. the location of the Saginaw River

  Ⓐ encyclopedia   Ⓒ *Readers' Guide*

  Ⓑ thesaurus   Ⓓ atlas

12. a recent article on toxic waste

  Ⓐ encyclopedia   Ⓒ *Readers' Guide*

  Ⓑ thesaurus   Ⓓ atlas

13. the life of Alexander the Great

  Ⓐ encyclopedia   Ⓒ *Readers' Guide*

  Ⓑ thesaurus   Ⓓ atlas

14. an article written by George Maliff

  Ⓐ encyclopedia   Ⓒ *Readers' Guide*

  Ⓑ thesaurus   Ⓓ atlas

15. a synonym for the word lovely

  Ⓐ encyclopedia   Ⓒ *Readers' Guide*

  Ⓑ thesaurus   Ⓓ atlas

16. the pronunciation of the word ptarmigan

  Ⓐ encyclopedia   Ⓒ dictionary

  Ⓑ thesaurus   Ⓓ almanac

17. the current population of the country of Botswana

  Ⓐ dictionary   Ⓒ almanac

  Ⓑ thesaurus   Ⓓ atlas

18. the rainfall amount for Death Valley last year

  Ⓐ dictionary   Ⓒ almanac

  Ⓑ encyclopedia   Ⓓ atlas

Unit 6 Test, p. 2

Darken the circle by the part of a book in which you would find the information.

19. the name of the author

   Ⓐ title page   Ⓒ table of contents

   Ⓑ copyright page   Ⓓ index

20. the page at the back of a book that lists where certain information can be found

   Ⓐ title page   Ⓒ table of contents

   Ⓑ copyright page   Ⓓ index

21. the date the book was published

   Ⓐ title page   Ⓒ table of contents

   Ⓑ copyright page   Ⓓ index

22. how many units are in the book

   Ⓐ title page   Ⓒ table of contents

   Ⓑ copyright page   Ⓓ index

Use the *Readers' Guide* samples to answer the questions.

HERTSGAARD, MARK
Onward and Upward with the Arts: Letting It Be.

KAGARLITSKY, BORIS
Make Them Truly Democratic.
The Nation 257:688–702 Dec '93

ICEBERGS
Icehunters. [International Ice Patrol; cover story] M. Dane. il map Popular Mechanics, 170:76–79 Oct '93

23. What article did Mark Hertsgaard write?

   Ⓐ "Onward and Upward with the Arts"

   Ⓑ "Icehunters"

   Ⓒ "Make Them Truly Democratic"

24. Which magazine has an article on icebergs?

   Ⓐ *New Yorker*

   Ⓑ *Popular Mechanics*

   Ⓒ *The Nation*

25. On which pages is the article by Boris Kagarlitsky?

   Ⓐ 688–702

   Ⓑ 170–176

   Ⓒ 76–79

26. Which article has a map?

   Ⓐ "Onward and Upward with the Arts"

   Ⓑ "Make Them Truly Democratic"

   Ⓒ "Icehunters"

Choose the correct answer for each question.

27. Which reference source does not use guide words?

   Ⓐ dictionary   Ⓑ atlas   Ⓒ encyclopedia

28. Which would you not use a dictionary to find?

   Ⓐ word origin   Ⓑ magazine articles   Ⓒ syllables

29. Which would you not find in a book?

   Ⓐ copyright page   Ⓑ table of contents   Ⓒ cross-reference

Answer Key

Assessment

Pages 7–10
1. H
2. A
3. S
4. S
5. lock
6. C
7. P
8. S
9. P
10. they will
11. we have
12. unhappy
13. b

The words in bold should be circled.
14. IM; (You); **Wait**
15. IN; you; **do believe**
16. E; I; **burned**
17. D; article; **made**
18. CP
19. CS
20. I
21. RO
22. CS
23. The word in bold should be labeled DO. [Before I left,] I ate a good **breakfast**.
24. Common nouns: citizens, city, position; Proper nouns: Mayor Dumonte, Ms. Lopez
25. The words in bold should be circled. nurse, **Ms. Abram**
26. future
27. present
28. past
29. are, were
30. saw, knew
31. begun, went
32. threw, broke
33. b
34. IP, **Somebody**
35. OP, **her**
36. PP, **their**
37. SP, **We**

The words in bold should be circled.
38. **jets**, their
39. adjective
40. adverb
41. adverb
42. adjective

The words in bold should be circled.
43. **on** the bus, **at** me, while

Letter:

956 E. Garden Circle
Bowman, TX 78787
April 13, 2007

Dear Steve,

We're so excited you're coming to visit! Even little Scott managed to say, "Uncle Steve visit," which was pretty good for a child of only twenty-two months, wouldn't you agree? Oh, I want to be sure I have the information correct. Please let me know as soon as possible if any of this is wrong: flight 561 arrives at 3:10 P.M. on May 22. See you then.

Your sister,
Amanda

44. Sentence order: 3, 1, 4, 2
45. b
46. Although the decision to close Mayfield Park was unpopular, it proved to be the correct choice.
47. adjective
48. before
49. Middle English
50. jol-ly
51. *Readers' Guide*
52. atlas
53. dictionary
54. encyclopedia
55. the Cree
56. in the forest hunting and trapping
57. southwest into buffalo country
58. Native Americans

Unit 1

Page 11
Answers will vary.

Page 12
1. two, past
2. too, to
3. hear
4. heard
5. not, know, not
6. seem, our
7. won, medal
8. weigh
9. air, so, need
10. rows
11. knew, new, feet
12. beet
13. not, scene
14. waist
15. piece
16. alter
17. too or two
18. weigh or whey
19. beach
20. plane
21. course
22. seam
23. new
24. sail
25. so or sow
26. brake
27. weak
28. rain or reign
29. bear
30. seen
31. might
32. hole
33. horse
34. forth
35. night
36. him
37. threw
38. groan
39. rap
40. pray
41. straight
42. soul
43. here
44. where or wear

Page 13
1. b
2. b
3. a
4. b
5. checkers
6. duck
7. can
8. alight
9. stall
10. snap
11. squash
12. quack
13. punch

Page 14
Words and meanings will vary.

Page 15
Words and meanings will vary.

Page 16
1. didn't
2. wasn't
3. we're
4. isn't
5. who's
6. hadn't
7. I'll
8. I'm
9. it's
10. don't
11. they've
12. wouldn't
13. won't
14. doesn't
15. weren't
16. there's
17. couldn't
18. I've
19. she'll
20. they're
21. They're; They are
22. They'll; They will
23. it's; it is
24. Mary's; Mary is
25. she'll; she will
26. doesn't; does not; he's; he is
27. He'd; He would
28. would've; would have
29. aren't; are not; Thom's; Thom is
30. they've; they have

Page 17
1.–12. Students should list any twelve of the following words: airline, understand, airport, seaport, air-condition, underground, sandpaper, undersea, doorknob, blackbird, underline, blackberry, doorway, seabird.
13.–18. Answers will vary.

Page 18
1. N
2. +
3. N
4. –
5. N
6. –
7. N
8. +
9. –
10. N
11. horrible
12. exciting
13. unpleasant
14. old
15. mature
16. over the hill

Page 19

1.–9. Meanings and definitions will vary.
1. in hot water
2. was beside herself
3. put their heads together
4. was all ears
5. throw in the towel
6. hit the road
7. eat crow
8. burn the midnight oil
9. cut me down to size

Unit 1 Test
Pages 20–21

1. B	13. B	25. C
2. C	14. A	26. B
3. A	15. C	27. A
4. D	16. D	28. C
5. C	17. B	29. B
6. A	18. A	30. C
7. D	19. C	31. D
8. B	20. D	32. B
9. C	21. B	33. A
10. B	22. D	34. B
11. A	23. B	35. A
12. D	24. A	36. D

Unit 2
Page 22

S should precede the following sentences, and students should end each with a period: 1, 3, 5, 7, 10, 13, 14, 16, 17, 22, 23, 25, 28, 29, 30.

Pages 23–24

1. D	22. IN
2. IM	23. IM
3. IN	24. E
4. IM	25. IN
5. IN	26. IM or E
6. IN	27. IM
7. D	28. D
8. IN	29. IM
9. IM	30. E
10. E	31. IM
11. IM	32. D
12. IN	33. IN
13. IN	34. IM
14. D	35. IM
15. IN	36. D
16. IM	37. D
17. IN	38. IN
18. IM	39. E
19. IN	40. IN
20. IM or E	41. D
21. D	42. E or IM

Students should circle the following sentences:
43. When will the train arrive? IN
44. It is delayed by bad weather. D
45. Juan and Shelly are on it. D
46. I haven't seen them in two years! E
47. They will stay with us for two weeks. D
48. We have many things planned for them. D
49. They will sleep in the guest room. D
50. Juan used to work at a zoo. D
51. Go in the reptile house. IM
52. Each elephant had a name. D
53. The elephants liked to train with Juan. D
54. Sandra, the elephant, had a baby. D
55. What did the zoo officials name the baby? IN
56. They surprised Juan! E

Pages 25–26

1. Amy / built
2. cleaner / will
3. waltzes / were
4. Victoria / ruled
5. people / are
6. visit / was
7. rocket / was
8. meeting / was
9. farmers / are
10. house / has
11. heart / pumps
12. computer / will
13. friend / has
14. silence / fell
15. officers / were
16. chef / prepared
17. father / is
18. Salazar / is
19. Lightning / struck
20. bicycling / are
21. They / answered
22. twilight / came
23. William / has
24. country / has
25. We / will
26. Butterflies / flew
27. bus / was
28.–53. Sentences will vary.

Page 27

1. plants / sprouted
2. program / was
3. I / used
4. truck / is
5. beavers / created
6. books / lined
7. Hail / pounded
8. I / bought
9. subject / is
10. bird / sang
11. trunk / was
12. sidewalk / had

Words in bold should be underlined twice.
13. vase / **was**
14. children / **had played**
15. group / **went**
16. He / **drove**
17. water-skiers / **were**
18. Birds / **have**
19. Who / **discovered**
20. I / **am reading**
21. headlights / **blinded**
22. page / **is**

Page 28

Words in bold should be underlined twice.

1. The sunken treasure ship **was** where?
2. Several sailboats **were** beyond the bridge.
3. No one **is** in that room.
4. The shouts of the victorious team **came** from the gymnasium.
5. Beautiful flowers **grew** beside the walk.
6. The surprise party **is** when?
7. (You) **Bring** your sales report to the meeting.
8. Only three floats **were** in the parade.
9. The bark of the dog **came** from the yard.
10. (You) **Place** the forks to the left of the plate.

Page 29

1. CS; I / often
2. SS; Sandy / left
3. CS; I / will
4. CS; Delhi / were
5. SS; fire / spread
6. CS; Lenora / helped
7. CS; hiking / were
8. CS; Sydney / are
9. CS; I / had
10. CS; Sea / are
11. CS; Democrats / made
12. SS; people / waved
13. CS; Jim / crated
14. CS; appearance / are
15. CS; dog / are
16. CS; Justin / are
17. SS; Tom / combed
18. CS; trees / bloom
19. SS; I / hummed
20. CS; antelope / once
21. CS; Hiroshi / raked
22. CS; Rouge / are
23. SS; gliding / is
24. SS; class / went
25. SS; doctor / asked
26.–27. Sentences will vary.

Page 30

1. CP; Edward / grinned
2. SP; Plants / need
3. SP; teakettles / were
4. CP; sister / buys
5. SP; Snow / covered
6. CP; Mr. Sanders / designs
7. SP; Popcorn / is
8. SP; Soccer / is
9. CP; ducks / quickly
10. CP; They / came
11. SP; Crystal / participated
12. CP; Josie / raked
13. CP; Perry / built
14. SP; We / collected
15. SP; Doug / arrived
16. SP; parents / are
17. SP; Herreras / live
18. CP; shingles / were
19. CP; audience / talked
20. CP; Automobiles / crowd
21. SP; pears / are
22. CP; group / grumbled
23. CP; She / worked
24. SP; Ichiro / collects
25. SP; supervisor / has
26.–27. Sentences will vary.

Page 31

Sentences may vary.
1. Lightning and thunder are parts of a thunderstorm.
2. Thunderstorms usually happen in the spring and bring heavy rains.
3. Depending on how close or far away it is, thunder sounds like a sharp crack or rumbles.
4. Lightning is very exciting to watch and can be very dangerous.
5. Lightning causes many fires and harms many people.
6. An open field or a golf course is an unsafe place to be during a thunderstorm.

Language: Usage and Practice 7, SV 1419027840

7. Benjamin Franklin wanted to protect <u>people</u> from lightning and invented the <u>lightning rod</u>.
8. A lightning rod is a <u>metal rod</u> placed on the <u>top</u> of a building and connected to the <u>ground</u> by a <u>cable</u>.

Page 32
The words in bold should be labeled DO.
1. <u>can carry</u>, **logs**
2. <u>made</u>, **rack**
3. <u>Do</u>, <u>plan</u>, **schedule**
4. <u>won</u>, **game**
5. <u>baked</u>, **pie**
6. <u>tuned</u>, **piano**
7. <u>take</u>, **lessons**
8. <u>composed</u>, **melody**
9. <u>enjoy</u>, **stories**
10. <u>orbited</u>, **moon**
11. <u>bought</u>, **coat**
12. <u>Did</u>, <u>find</u>, **glasses**
13. <u>drove</u>, **truck**
14. <u>shrugged</u>, **shoulders**
15. <u>have finished</u>, **work**
16. <u>drink</u>, **milk**
17. <u>can solve</u>, **problem**
18. <u>made</u>, **flag**
19. <u>will learn</u>, **something**
20. <u>needs</u>, **friends**
21. <u>have found</u>, **dime**
22. <u>ate</u>, **apple**

Page 33
The words in bold should be labeled DO, and the words underlined twice should be labeled IO.
1. <u>give</u>, <u>Red Sea</u>, **color**
2. <u>gave</u>, <u>cashier</u>, **check**
3. <u>showed</u>, <u>audience</u>, **tricks**
4. <u>taught</u>, <u>them</u>, **rules**
5. <u>brought</u>, <u>us</u>, **coins**
6. <u>will give</u>, <u>reader</u>, **pleasure**
7. <u>Have</u>, <u>written</u>, <u>brother</u>, **letter**
8. <u>made</u>, <u>us</u>, **sandwiches**
9. <u>gave</u>, <u>Mission Control</u>, **data**
10. <u>bought</u>, <u>friend</u>, **etching**
11. <u>did</u>, <u>sell</u>, <u>Mike</u>, **car**
12. <u>have given</u>, <u>dog</u>, **scrubbing**
13. <u>Give</u>, <u>usher</u>, **ticket**
14. <u>brought</u>, <u>brother</u>, **ring**
15. <u>Hand</u>, <u>me</u>, **pencil**
16. <u>gave</u>, <u>orchestra</u>, **break**
17. <u>Show</u>, <u>me</u>, **picture**
18. <u>have given</u>, <u>you</u>, **money**
19. <u>Give</u>, <u>Leeza</u>, **message**
20. <u>gave</u>, <u>town</u>, **statue**

Page 34
The following clauses should be underlined.
1. Frank will be busy
2. I have only one hour
3. The project must be finished
4. Gloria volunteered to do the typing
5. The work is going too slowly
6. I didn't think we could finish
7. What else should we do
8. you can type it
9. we completed the project
10. We actually got it finished
11. who went shopping
12. which is a mountain bike
13. when the sale was over
14. because she wanted some new things
15. since he went late
16. where we went shopping
17. who own the stores
18. which is miles away
19. because the bus was coming
20. because we had run fast

Page 35
The following clauses should be underlined.
1. that always points northward
2. that measures earthquake tremors
3. who work in science laboratories today
4. that she has played in that position
5. whose wrist was broken
6. that I caught
7. that contains a subordinate clause
8. that I promised to show you
9. that I read
10.–15. Sentences will vary.

Page 36
The following clauses should be underlined.
1. when the cloudy skies cleared
2. Although the weather was mild and sunny
3. after we arrived at the park
4. because we were prepared
5. Since we had our jackets
6. Although the clouds remained
7. when we got to the top of the hill
8. After enjoying the beauty and the quiet for a while
9. since it was still early
10. because we were so relaxed and happy
11.–16. Sentences will vary.

Page 37
Sentences 2, 3, 5, and 8 are simple sentences.
Sentences 1, 4, 6, and 7 are compound sentences.
9. [You ... rules,] or [you ... race.]
10. [I ... test,] and [Maria ... too.]
11. [Shall ... box,] or [do ... here?]
12. [We ... freedom,] or [an ... us.]
13. [He ... pass,] but [no ... it.]
14. [The ... cut,] but [he ... stitches.]
15. [I ... home,] but [the ... travel.]
16. [The ... over,] and [everyone ... year.]
17. [The ... hardship,] yet [they ... had.]
18. [Move ... here] ; [I'll ... it.]
19. [Candace ... football] ; [Jarrett ... soccer.]
20. [I ... safely,] and [I ... belts.]
21. [Please ... number,] and [I'll ... work.]

Page 38
1. The <u>shadows</u> [that ... trees] <u>were</u> a deep purple.
2. The <u>soldiers</u> <u>waded</u> across the stream [where ... shallow.]
3. <u>They</u> <u>waited</u> for me [until ... came.]
4. The <u>fans</u> of that team <u>were</u> sad [when ... game.]
5. [When ... here,] <u>he</u> <u>was charmed</u> by the beauty of the hills.
6. <u>Sophia</u> <u>will call</u> for you [when ... ready.]
7. Some <u>spiders</u> [that ... Sumatra] <u>have</u> legs seventeen inches long.
8. <u>Those</u> [who ... going] <u>will arrive</u> on time.
9. <u>Do</u> not <u>throw</u> the bat [after ... ball.]
10. <u>Tell</u> us about the trip [that ... ago.]
11.–16. Sentences will vary.

Page 39
Sentences will vary. Check that students have corrected the run-on sentences.

Page 40
Expanded sentences will vary.

Unit 2 Test
Pages 41–42

1. C	11. B	21. B
2. B	12. C	22. A
3. A	13. A	23. A
4. D	14. C	24. D
5. C	15. A	25. B
6. B	16. C	26. C
7. A	17. B	27. C
8. A	18. A	28. B
9. C	19. A	
10. C	20. B	

Unit 3
Page 43
1. Lupe Garcia; years; supervisor
2. piece; land; mouth; river; delta
3. Gilbert Stuart; artist; portraits; presidents
4. Albert Einstein; scientist; Germany
5. library; world; Alexandria; Egypt
6. Jim Thorpe; Oklahoma; athletes; time
7. Mahalia Jackson; singer; spirituals
8. Marconi; telegraph
9. parades; games; television; New Year's Day
10. Terry Fox; runner; leg; cancer; miles; Canada
11. *Boston News-Letter*; newspaper; United States

Language: Usage and Practice 7, SV 1419027840

12. message; English Channel; century
13. Chicago; city; Lake Michigan
14. seat; window
15. Kuang; car
16. children; trip; Carlsbad Caverns
17. Washington; D.C.; capital; United States
18. France; food; country; Europe
19. Maria; saxophone
20. Hailstones; raindrops; snowflakes
21. nights; summer
22. rivers; explorers
23. Jeff; carport; boat
24. California; home; stars
25. William Caxton; book; England
26. Chris; tomatoes; lettuce; cherries; market
27. building; offices; stores; apartments
28. Laticia; Peoria; Illinois; friend
29. airport; hours; snowstorm
30. pen; ink

Pages 44–45
Words in bold should be circled; other words should be underlined.
1. story; prince; pauper; clothing
2. **New York**; **Los Angeles**; cities; **United States**
3. story; **Scrooge**; **Tiny Tim**
4. **Sumatra**; island; **Indian Ocean**
5. **United States**; hail; damage; tornadoes
6. paper; **Chinese**
7. "Rikki-tikki-tavi"; **Rudyard Kipling**; story; mongoose
8. *Shamrock*; name; emblem; **Ireland**
9. shilling; coin; **England**
10. lights; car; pavement
11. **Nathan**; **Samuel**; **Tuesday**
12. **Great Sphinx**; monument; **Egypt**
13. family; **Mexico**; **Canada**; year
14.–61. Answers will vary.

Pages 46–47
1. brushes
2. lunches
3. countries
4. benches
5. earrings
6. calves
7. pianos
8. foxes
9. daisies
10. potatoes
11. dishes
12. stores
13. booklets
14. tomatoes
15. trucks
16. chefs
17. branches
18. toddlers
19. pennies
20. echoes
21. pieces
22. doors
23. islands
24. cherries
25. houses
26. garages
27. fish
28. watches
29. elves
30. desks
31. pans
32. sheep
33. gardens
34. ponies
35. solos
36. trees
37. lights
38. churches
39. cities
40. spoonfuls
41. vacations
42. homes
43. apples, oranges, boxes
44. letters, friends
45. buildings, elevators
46. families, miles, lakes
47. tops, cars, storms
48. aunts, uncles

Pages 48–49
1. brother's
2. boy's
3. Carol's
4. children's
5. grandmother's
6. men's
7. heroes'
8. women's
9. ox's
10. man's
11. Dr. Kahn's
12. soldier's
13. pony's
14. friend's
15. child's
16. engineers'
17. birds'
18. Jon's
19.–28. Sentences will vary.
29. doctor's
30. senator's
31. sheep's
32. baby's
33. instructor's
34. collectors'
35. spider's
36. Mr. Takata's
37. Chet's
38. Lawanda's
39. Carl Sandburg's
40. child's
41. women's
42. elephants'
43. sister's
44. Brazil's
45. friends'
46. bird's
47. children's
48. owl's
49. brothers'
50. student's
51. country's
52. owner's
53. uncle's
54. Jolene's
55. men's

Page 50
Words in bold should be circled; other words should be underlined.
1. **Banff**, the large Canadian national park
2. **painter**, Vincent Van Gogh
3. **The White House**, home of the President of the United States
4. **Uncle Marco**, my mother's brother
5. **Earth**, the only inhabited planet in our solar system
6. **scorpion**, a native of the southwestern part of North America
7. **cat**, Amelia
8. **Judge Andropov**, the presiding judge
9. **friend**, Luisa
10.–18. Answers will vary.

Page 51
1. Watch
2. dusted
3. copy
4. burned
5. fell
6. play
7. practiced
8. dashed
9. expresses
10. enjoys
11. leads
12. snowed
13. hiked
14. made
15. hand
16. Draw
17. skated
18. answered
19. repaired
20. suffered
21. Write
22. moved
23. worked
24. directs
25. played
26. walked
27. helped
28. collapsed
29. ticked

Page 52
1. appears   6. are
2. is   7. smell
3. was   8. feels
4. is   9. sounds
5. looks   10. seems
11.–20. Answers will vary.

Page 53
1. is stopping; stopped; (have, has, had) stopped
2. is listening; listened; (have, has, had) listened
3. is carrying; carried; (have, has, had) carried
4. is helping; helped; (have, has, had) helped
5. is starting; started; (have, has, had) started
6. is borrowing; borrowed; (have, has, had) borrowed
7. is calling; called; (have, has, had) called
8. is receiving; received; (have, has, had) received
9. is hoping; hoped; (have, has, had) hoped
10. is illustrating; illustrated; (have, has, had) illustrated
11. is dividing; divided; (have, has, had) divided

Language: Usage and Practice 7, SV 1419027840

12. is changing; changed; (have, has, had) changed
13. is scoring; scored; (have, has, had) scored
14. is ironing; ironed; (have, has, had) ironed
15. is studying; studied; (have, has, had) studied
16. is collecting; collected; (have, has, had) collected
17. is laughing; laughed; (have, has, had) laughed

Page 54
1.–10. Sentences will vary.
11. has returned
12. has planned
13. would have answered
14. have been looking
15. have asked
16. have organized
17. has been planned
18. must speak
19. were dimmed
20. had been seen
21. were threatened
22. are planning

Page 55
1.–8. Sentences will vary.
9. future
10. past
11. future
12. present
13. past
14. past
15. present
16. future
17. past
18. past

Page 56
1. past perfect
2. past perfect
3. present perfect
4. past perfect
5. present perfect
6. present perfect
7. present perfect
8. past perfect
9. present perfect
10. present perfect
11. has
12. have
13. had
14. has
15. had
16. has
17. had

Page 57
1. is
2. are
3. is
4. is
5. are
6. is
7. are
8. Are
9. is
10. are
11. were; was
12. were
13. was
14. were
15. were
16. weren't
17. weren't
18. were
19. weren't
20. were
21. was
22. was
23. was
24. Were
25. were
26. Weren't
27. were
28. Were
29. were

Page 58
1. took
2. taken
3. wrote
4. written
5. gave
6. given
7. written
8. written
9. given
10. wrote
11. taken
12. taken
13. gave
14. took
15. given
16. written
17. took
18. gave
19. written
20. took
21. written
22. gave
23. given
24. taken
25. took
26. gave
27. taken

Page 59
1. saw
2. gone
3. began
4. went
5. begun
6. seen
7. gone
8. saw
9. seen
10. went
11. begun
12. began
13. gone
14. began
15. begun
16. saw
17. went
18. seen
19. went
20. began
21. began
22.–27. Sentences will vary.

Page 60
1. worn
2. chosen
3. broke
4. rose
5. stolen
6. chosen
7. worn
8. rose
9. stolen
10. rose
11. worn
12. chose
13. broken
14. stolen
15. risen
16. broken
17. wore
18. risen
19. stole
Paragraph: Students should circle the following verbs: had rose, had stole, worn, chosen, had broke.

Page 61
1. drank
2. rung
3. drunk
4. knew
5. thrown
6. come
7. rang
8. known
9. threw
10. came
11. drunk
12. come
13. knew
14. thrown
15. come
16. rang
17. drank
18.–26. Sentences will vary.

Page 62
1. drawn
2. driven; began
3. fallen
4. eaten; ran
5. drew
6. run
7. fallen; ran
8. fallen
9. drove
10. eaten
11. ate
12. fallen
13. ran
14. drove
15. drew
16. fallen
17. fell

18. driven
19. ran
20. ate
21. eaten
22. drawn
23. run

Page 63
1. doesn't
2. did
3. done
4. doesn't
5. did
6. Don't
7. done
8. Don't
9. doesn't
10. don't
11. done
12. did
13. Doesn't
14. Doesn't
15. done
16. doesn't
17.–20. Sentences will vary.

Page 64
1. joined; T
2. wanted; T
3. exercised; I
4. became; I
5. worked; I
6. preferred; T
7. liked; T
8. switched; T
9. took; T
10. used; T
11. swam; I
12. was; T
13. had; T
14. splashed; I
Words in bold should be circled.
15. walked; **Tiny**
16. pulled; **Carlos**
17. washed; **Tiny**
18. loved; **water**
19. splashed; **Carlos**
20. loved; **bones**
21. chewed; **bones**
22. found; **Tiny**

Pages 65–66
1. to quit
2. to finish
3. to run
4. to win
5. to finish
6. to accomplish
7. to see
8. yelling
9. excited
10. running

Language: Usage and Practice 7, SV 1419027840

11. marching
12. Chosen
13. flashing
14. interested
15. Studying
16. reading
17. Learning
18. Memorizing
19. Remembering
20. studying
21. Dancing
22. infinitive; To act
23. gerund; Acting
24. infinitive; To write
25. gerund; Working
26. infinitive; to participate
27. participle; hurried
28. participle; moving
29. infinitive; to read
30. gerund; Auditioning
31. participle; stirring
32. gerund; Rehearsing
33. infinitive; to memorize
34. participle; convincing
35. gerund; performing
36. participle; smiling
37. infinitive; To act
38. participle; budding
39. gerund; Performing
40. gerund; Bowing
41. gerund; playing
42. infinitive; To continue
43. gerund; Acting
44. participle; Interrupted
45. gerund; acting
46. infinitive; to excel
47. participle; Well-rehearsed

Page 67
1. A
2. A
3. A
4. A
5. P
6. A
7. P
8. P
9. P
10. A
11.–16. Sentences will vary.

Pages 68–69
1. me
2. them
3. me
4. my
5. he
6. she
7. they
8. us
9. her
10. someone
11. I
12. your
13. He
14. me
15. Who
16. they

17. Everyone
18. their
19. Whom
20. she
21. hers
22. Who
23. ours
24. who
25. I; you; him; our
26. Who
27. They; us; we; their
28. you; me; I; them
29. He; us
30. My; our
31. Whom; you
32. you; me
33. They; us
34. his
35. Who; them
36. She; my; who
37. mine
38. Someone; them
39. Who; she
40. She; us
41. who
42. she; you
43. Who; me
44. we; them
45. Which; your
46. I; you; our
47. Which; mine
48. you; your
49. you; us
50. anybody
51. You; I
52. you; him
53.–57. Sentences will vary.

Page 70
Students should circle the words in bold; other words should be underlined.
1. **Micah**; he
2. **Carmen**; her
3. **Carmen**; her
4. **Micah**; his
5. **Carmen**; her; **math**; it
6. **Micah and Carmen**; they
7. **test**; it
8. **class**; its
9. **palms**; they
10. **teacher**; he
11. **test**; it
12. **student**; his or her; **test**; it
13. **tests**; them
14. **Carmen**; her
15. their
16. him
17. its
18. his
19. they

20. his
21. its
22. their
23. her
24. their

Page 71
1.–5. Adjectives will vary.
6. This; old; comfortable
7. a; funny
8. This; heavy; many; dangerous
9. The; eager; odd; every
10. The; tired; thirsty
11. This; favorite
12. The; solitary; the; lonely
13. the; sixth
14. These; damp
15. French
16. those
17. A; red; the; tall
18. The; heavy
19. A; tour; the; pirate's
20. The; gorgeous; Italian
21. fresh
22. mashed; baked
23. Chinese

Page 72
1. those
2. That
3. those
4. those
5. That
6. Those
7. those
8. those
9. these
10. those
11. these
12. these
13. those
14. this
15. Those
16. these
17. those
18. That
19. These
20. those
21. these
22. these
23. These
24. those
25. Those

Page 73
1. more changeable
2. most faithful
3. more agreeable
4. busiest
5. longer
6. loveliest
7. freshest
8. higher
9. more enjoyable
10. most reckless
11. youngest
12. tallest
13. more difficult
14. quietest

Page 74
1. slowly; clearly; expressively
2. too; recklessly
3. slowly; quickly
4. too; harshly

5. here
6. everywhere
7. suddenly; quickly; around
8. too; rapidly
9. well
10. soundly
11. noisily
12. early
13. severely
14. quickly; steadily
15.–24. Adverbs will vary.

Page 75
1. sooner
2. soonest
3. hard
4. more
5. faster
6. most
7. fastest
8. faster
9. more seriously
10. most frequently
11. more quickly
12. most promptly
13. more promptly
14. most eagerly
15. more carefully
16. hardest

Page 76
1. of
2. of
3. in
4. For
5. At; to; about
6. of
7. beside
8. of
9. to; at; of
10. in; in
11. of; during; of
12. of; at
13. at; near
14. on; for
15. with
16. behind
17. in
18. of; on; behind
19. to; during
20. down
21. across; in
22. over; into
23. of; under
24. below; of
25. behind
26. of; by
27. between
28. for

Language: Usage and Practice 7, SV 1419027840

Page 77
Students should circle the words in bold.
1. (above the **clouds**)
2. (to **North Carolina**)
3. (on the second **block**)
4. (on that **hill**)
5. (on the wet **pavement**)
6. (in the seventeenth **century**)
7. (by the **Romans**)
8. (in **1781**)
9. (from **Asia**)
10. (into the **street**)
11. (in a **pen**)
12. (over the **fence**)
13. (in **Denver, Colorado**)
14. (to **North America**)
15. (under the **shade**) (of the giant elm **tree**)
16. (by a scuba **diver**)
17. (of **soldiers**) (behind the **tank**)
18. (across the **stream**)
19. (across the **nation**)
20. (into the **sack**)
21. (up the **pole**)
22. (in **Nova Scotia**)
23. (to our **region**)
24. (in the **Adirondack Mountains**)
25. (behind a parked **car**)

Page 78
1. to the ranch; adverb
2. in France; adverb
3. in Tennessee; adjective
4. to the public library; adverb
5. in an old house; adverb
6. with red trim; adjective
7. in the zoo; adjective
8. in Asia; adverb
9. of my money; adjective
10. over the hat; adverb
11. of a Sequoia tree trunk; adjective
12. of New York; adjective
13. near the docks; adverb
14. to the movie; adverb
15. in 1911; adverb
16. in this room; adjective
17. across the yard; adverb
18. of petrified wood; adjective
19. across the lawn; adverb

Page 79
1. whether
2. and
3. when
4. or
5. and
6. unless
7. or
8. and
9. and
10. because
11. but
12. and
13. because
14. since
15. but
16. Although
17. than
18. neither/nor
19. either/or
20. but
21. for
22. while
23. not only/but also
24. either/or
25. neither/nor
26. Neither/nor

Unit 3 Test
Pages 80–81

1. B	15. C	29. B
2. A	16. A	30. A
3. A	17. A	31. B
4. B	18. C	32. C
5. A	19. C	33. A
6. C	20. C	34. C
7. A	21. A	35. B
8. C	22. A	36. C
9. A	23. C	37. A
10. A	24. C	38. B
11. B	25. D	39. C
12. A	26. B	40. C
13. B	27. C	41. B
14. C	28. A	42. A

Unit 4
Pages 82–84
Students should circle and capitalize the first letter in each of the following words:
1. What
2. Francis; The; Star; Spangled; Banner
3. Edgar; The; Raven
4. Paul; When
5. Who; Snowbound; The; Barefoot; Boy
6. What; Give
7. Miami; Florida; Atlanta; Georgia
8. Potomac; River; Virginia; Maryland
9. *Pinta*; *Niña*; *Santa*; *Maria*; Columbus
10. Spanish; Mississippi; River; English; Jamestown
11. American; Red; Cross; Clara; Barton
12. Rocky; Mountains; Andes; Mountains; Alps
13. Dr.; Thompson
14. Mayor; Thomas
15. Dr.; Crawford; W.; Long
16. Mr.; Mrs.; Randall
17. Senator; Dixon
18. Gov.; Alden
19. Ms.; Howell
20. Niles School Art Fair / Sat., Feb. 8th, 9 A.M. / 110 N. Elm Dr.
21. Shoreville Water Festival / June 23–24 / Mirror Lake / Shoreville, MN 55108
22. October Fest / October 28 and 29 / 9 A.M.–5 P.M. / 63 Maple St.
23. Barbara Dumont / 150 Telson Rd. / Markham, Ontario L3R 1E5
24. Captain C. J. Neil / c/o *Ocean Star* / P. 0. Box 4455 / Portsmouth, NH 03801
25. Dr. Charles B. Stevens / Elmwood Memorial Hospital / 1411 First Street / Tucson, AZ 85062
26.–39. Sentences will vary.

Pages 85–86

1. ?	8. ?
2. .	9. .
3. ?	10. .
4. ?	11. ?
5. .	12. .
6. .	13. ?
7. ?	14. ?

Paragraph:
   Did you know that experts say dogs have been around for thousands of years? In fact, they were the first animals to be made domestic. The ancestors of dogs were hunters. Wolves are related to domestic dogs. Like wolves, dogs are social animals and prefer to travel in groups. This is called pack behavior.
   There have been many famous dogs throughout history. Can you name any of them? In the eleventh century, one dog, Saur, was named king of Norway. The actual king was angry because his people had removed him from the throne, so he decided to make them subjects of the dog. The first dog in space was a Russian dog named Laika. Laika was aboard for the 1957 journey of *Sputnik*. Most people have heard of Rin Tin Tin and Lassie. These dogs became famous in movies and television.
   There are several hundred breeds of dogs throughout the world. The smallest is the Chihuahua. A Chihuahua weighs less than two pounds. Can you think of the largest? A Saint Bernard or a mastiff can weigh over 150 pounds.

15. .	24. .
16. .	25. .
17. !; . or !	26. !
18. !; .	27. ! or .
19. .	28. .
20. .	29. .
21. . or !	30. !
22. !	31. .
23. !; !; !	32. !; .

Paragraph: (Punctuation may vary.)
   Mr. Henry Modine lives in San Francisco, California. He often exclaims, "What a wonderful town!" What do you think he does for a living? Mr. Modine owns a fishing boat, *The Marlin*. In all of San Francisco, there are few boats as fine as *The Marlin*. (or !) Henry Modine named his boat after the fish his customers like the best—the marlin. Henry guarantees his customers a fish if they come out on his boat.
   "Fantastic!" shouts Henry when someone hooks a marlin. Henry then says, "Bring it in." Part of Henry's job is to help the fishers reel in the big fish. Can you believe that some marlins weigh 1,000 pounds or more? Most of the ones Henry's customers catch weigh about 100 pounds. They are either striped marlins or black marlins.

Pages 87–88

Students should place commas after words shown:
1. Frank, Mary,
2. anniversary,
3. with, members,
4. homes,
5. active, friendly,
6. work,
7. Knudsens,
8. together,
9. plans,"
10. said,
11. said,
12. asked,
13. can't,"
14. week,"
15. said,
16. record,"
17. it,"
18. out,"
19. Anthony, a grocery store owner,
20. "Diane,
21. "Of course, open,"
22. "Pierre, Elaine's, by,"
23. said, "Alicia,
24. "Yes,
25. asked, "Martin,
26. "Well, afternoon,"
27. Alvin, the butcher,
28. wait, Alvin,"
29. manager, Juan,
30. "Please, number,"
31. "Yes, usual,"
32. Martin, the produce manager,
33. Well,
34. left,"
35. cherries, bananas,
36. Sara,
37. cooking, baking,
38. Today, July 18,

Paragraph:

Men, women, boys, and girls from across the nation participate in the Special Olympics. Because of this event, patterned after the Olympic games, boys and girls with disabilities have opportunities to compete in a variety of sports. The Special Olympics includes competition in track, swimming, and gymnastics. Volunteers plan carefully, and they work hard to ensure that the event will be challenging, rewarding, and worthwhile for all the participants. One of my neighbors, Chris Bell, once worked as a volunteer. "It was an experience that I'll never forget," he said.

Page 89
1. "Wait for me," said Lora, "because ... you."
2. "Kim, ... spacecraft?" asked Kyle.
3. "Where ... desk?" inquired the stranger.
4. Joanne asked, "What ... address?"
5. Davis asked, "How ... Empire?"
6. "Carlos, ... article?" asked the teacher.
7. "Good morning," said Cindi.
8. Jasmine asked, "Did ... fell?"
9. "The ... minutes," said Rico.
10. "Hoan, you're early," said Melissa.
11. "Come on," said the coach, "you'll ... game!"
12. Shannon said, "I ... worker."
13. didn't; Shay's
14. Haven't; Darren's
15. didn't; Larry's
16. employees'; didn't

Page 90
1. 2:10
2. you:
3. 4:30
4. items:
5. following:
6. 8:00; 10:00
7. 3:00
8. garden-ing
9. old-fashioned
10. sign-up
11. Twenty-seven
12. daughter-in-law
13. audi-torium
14. well-known
15. long-term

Unit 4 Test
Pages 91–92

1. A	11. D	21. D
2. B	12. A	22. A
3. D	13. B	23. C
4. C	14. C	24. A
5. C	15. D	25. B
6. D	16. C	26. D
7. D	17. B	27. A
8. C	18. A	28. C
9. D	19. C	
10. A	20. D	

Unit 5
Page 93
Sentences will vary.

Page 94
1.–3. Students should underline the first sentence in each paragraph.
4.–5. Topic sentences will vary.
Topics and topic sentences will vary.

Page 95
Paragraph:
Students should circle the first sentence and underline the remaining sentences except "Theresa is very athletic."
1.–2. Details sentences will vary.
Details for topic sentence will vary.

Page 96
1. Chronological; first; Then; Finally
2. Spatial: next to; left; top; down
3. Order: 2, 3, 4, 1
Paragraphs will vary.

Page 97
1. c
2. d
3. a
4. b
5. c
6. b
7. d
8. a
9. c or d
10. b
11. A child protection dog and his handler will appear.
12.–13. Answers will vary.
Topics and audiences will vary.

Page 98
Answers will vary.

Page 99
Outlines will vary.

Page 100
1. Who
2. What
3. How or When
4. Where
5. Why
6. When
7.–13. Answers will vary.

Page 101
1. no
2. Sentences will vary.
3. Its facilities, which will include....
4. Questions will vary.
5. a small ice rink, meeting rooms, arts-and-crafts facilities, locker rooms with showers, and possibly a weight-lifting room

Pages 102–103

The Berryton City Council approved plans today for construction of a new recreation center. Mayor June Booth said, "The center, to be located on the site of the current Adams Park, will provide Berryton residents with a variety of recreational programs." The center's facilities will include an indoor pool, two gymnasiums, arts-and-crafts facilities, and a small ice rink. Several meeting rooms will also be included for use by various organizations.

Check that students have used the correct proofreader's marks.

Representatives from several community organizations attended the meeting to express their support of the recreation center. "Construction of this center is long overdue. Our members will now have a central place in which to meet, instead of crowding into each other's homes," said Milton Sayre, chairman of the Berryton Senior Citizens' League.

Plans call for a groundbreaking ceremony on Thursday, May 16, at 2:30, followed by a reception in Adams Park. Mayor Booth, Superintendent Jim Leland, and city council members will participate. All residents are invited to join them at the ceremony.

Unit 5 Test
Pages 104–105
1. B   7. B   13. A
2. D   8. D   14. C
3. D   9. C   15. D
4. C   10. D   16. D
5. B   11. C
6. C   12. B

Unit 6
Page 106
Students should check the following words:
1. faster, fetch, flag, fancy, fertile, flame
2. impossible, incomplete, immense, indeed, improve, infect, imagine
3. rail, ranch, raw, raft, ramp, rate, rake

Words should be numbered to appear in the following order:
4. beach, bear, bedroom, believe, benefit, biography, blame, blend, blink, block. Guide words: beach/block.
5. department, depend, dessert, determine, difference, dine, discard, disease, district, disturb. Guide words: department/disturb.
6. face, faint, fair, family, finger, fire, flavor, flower, follow, free. Guide words: face/free.

Page 107
1. al-low-ance
2. por-ridge
3. har-ness
4. ped-dle
5. char-ac-ter
6. hick-o-ry
7. so-lu-tion
8. va-ri-e-ty
9. tal-ent
10. weath-er
11. bril-liant
12. en-thu-si-asm
13. dra-mat-ic
14. em-ploy-ment

15. lab-o-ra-to-ry
16. judg-ment
17. king-dom
18. rec-og-nize
19. u-su-al
20. yes-ter-day
21.–28. Answers may vary. Suggested:
21. vic-torious, victori-ous
22. in-ferior, inferi-or
23. quan-tity, quanti-ty
24. sat-isfactory, satisfacto-ry
25. se-curity, securi-ty
26. pos-session, posses-sion
27. ther-mometer, thermome-ter
28. get-away, geta-way

Page 108
1. cage, costume
2. cotton
3. cotton
4. cotton
5. an outfit worn in pretending to be someone else
6.–8. Sentences will vary.

Page 109
1. guppy
2. emotion
3. Old French and Old English
4. load
5. marathon
6. emotion; line; load
7. to move away; disturb
8. He introduced the fish to England.
9. from the Old English word *lād*
10. because a messenger once ran from Marathon to Athens to announce a victory over the Persians
11. load
12. line
13. emotion; line

Page 110
1. index
2. title page
3. table of contents

4. copyright page
5. title page
6. copyright page
7. the Sioux
8. 6–9
9. 24–27
10. 14–17
11. buffalo
12. the Sioux today
13. yes
14. page 32

Page 111
1. 000–099
2. 500–599
3. 500–599
4. 100–199
5. 400–499
6. 600–699
7. 500–599
8. 000–099
9. 700–799
10. 800–899
11. 300–399
12. 900–999
13. 200–299
14. 000–099
15. 700–799
16.–18. Answers will vary.

Page 112
1. Answers will vary.
2. 1888–1931
3. Voss, Norway
4. The University of Notre Dame
5. being the head coach of Notre Dame's football team
6. Answers will vary.
7. the west coast of the United States
8. coast or California redwood
9. It grows extremely tall.
10. 200 to 275 feet
11.–16. Answers will vary.

Page 113
1. 1
2. 68
3. no
4. cocktail, dip, pickle and relish, spread
5. main food or ingredient

6. acorn squash
7. almonds and stuffed celery
8. flour
9. appetizer(s)
10. cheese ball
11. peanut flour

Page 114
1. Dave Berkman
2. *US News and World Report*
3. A. Comarow
4. *Television Quarterly*
5. television
6. 63–69
7. 115
8. November 1993
9. il
10. October 1993

Page 115
1. encyclopedia
2. *Readers' Guide*
3. atlas or encyclopedia
4. dictionary
5. almanac
6. atlas
7. thesaurus
8. dictionary
9. *Readers' Guide*
10. dictionary
11. encyclopedia
12. thesaurus
13. encyclopedia
14. *Readers' Guide*
15. almanac
16. dictionary

Pages 116–117
Answers will vary.

Unit 6 Test
Page 118–119
1. A   11. D   21. B
2. A   12. C   22. C
3. B   13. A   23. A
4. C   14. C   24. B
5. A   15. B   25. A
6. C   16. C   26. C
7. A   17. C   27. B
8. B   18. C   28. B
9. B   19. A   29. C
10. D or A   20. D

CPSIA information can be obtained
at www.ICGtesting.com
Printed in the USA
LVHW021050030822
725067LV00007B/185